THUDDING DRUMS

THUDDING DRUMS

An Anthology of English and
South African Poetry

COMPILED BY

G. M. MILLER

THE SCHOOL, PLUMTREE, SOUTHERN RHODESIA

UNIVERSITY OF LONDON PRESS LTD.

WARWICK SQUARE, LONDON, E.C.4

First Printed 1942
Fourth Impression 1953

AGENTS OVERSEAS

AUSTRALIA
(*and its Dependencies*)
W. S. SMART   P.O. Box 120, SYDNEY, N.S.W.
Showroom: 558, George Street.

CANADA
CLARKE, IRWIN & CO., LTD.,
103, St. Clair Avenue West, TORONTO, 5.

EGYPT AND THE SUDAN
DINO JUDAH NAHUM   P.O. Box 940, CAIRO
Showroom: 44, Sharia Sherif Pasha.

FAR EAST
(*including China and Japan*)
DONALD MOORE   Oldham Hall, SINGAPORE, 9.

INDIA, PAKISTAN, BURMA AND CEYLON
ORIENT LONGMANS, LTD.,
BOMBAY: Nicol Road, Ballard Estate.
CALCUTTA: 17, Chittaranjan Ave.
MADRAS: 36A, Mount Road.

NEW ZEALAND
(*and its Dependencies*)
R. J. SARE   41, Shortland Street, AUCKLAND, C.1.

SOUTH AFRICA
H. B. TIMMINS   P.O. Box 94, CAPE TOWN.
Showroom: 58–60, Long Street.

Printed & Bound in England for the UNIVERSITY OF LONDON PRESS LTD.,
by HAZELL, WATSON & VINEY, LTD., Aylesbury and London

PREFACE

THE present volume is offered to the schools of Rhodesia and the Union of South Africa in the hope that it will add something to the pleasure and interest of their poetry lessons. Much of it reflects their own familiar environment. If those who read it find that it has brought new and beautiful associations to the common round of their own experience, its purpose will have been achieved. Perhaps, too, they will discover that they can point with pride to the work of their own South African poets.

G. M. M.

PLUMTREE, 1942.

CONTENTS

(The numbers of the poems are given in brackets)

14

ACKNOWLEDGMENTS

FOR permission to reproduce copyright poems, Mr. G. M. Miller and the publishers tender their grateful thanks to:

Messrs. Jonathan Cape Ltd. for " Thunderstorms " from *The Poems of W. H. Davies*; for " The Pylons " from *Green Legacy*, by Stanley Snaith, for " Out of the Ark " and " The Albatross " from *The Flaming Terrapin*, by Roy Campbell; Messrs. Macmillan & Co. Ltd. with the Trustees of the Hardy Estate for " Shelley's Skylark," " The Oxen " and " In Time of ' The Breaking of Nations,' " from *The Collected Poems of Thomas Hardy*, with Mr. Francis Carey Slater for songs and extracts from *The Trek*, with Mr. Lance Fallaw for " Simon Van Der Stel " from *Silverleaf and Oak*, for " The Rose Tree " from *The Collected Poems of W. B. Yeats*, with the Executrix of the late Rudyard Kipling for " Puck's Song " from *Puck of Pook's Hill*; Mr. W. J. Turner for " The Forest Bird," " The Lion " and " India " from *Selected Poems* (Oxford University Press) ; Messrs. Faber & Faber for poems by Roy Campbell from *Adamastor* and for " The Express," by Stephen Spender; and to Mr. Walter de la Mare for " The Scribe " and " England," with Messrs. Longmans, Green & Co. for " The Rainbow " and " Portrait of a Warrior " from *Songs of Childhood*.

To Mr. Robert Graves for " The Poets " from *Collected Poems* (Messrs. Cassell & Co.); Messrs. Gerald Duckworth & Co. Ltd. for "Winter the Huntsman," by Osbert Sitwell; The Richards Press Ltd. for " Twelfth Night," by W. R. Childe from *Neo-Georgian Poetry, 1936–37*; Mrs. B. Ayrton-Gould for " Beauty the Pilgrim," by Gerald Gould; the Executors of the late A. E. Housman for " Cherry Trees "; The Oxford University Press with the Rev. Arthur Shearly Cripps for poems from *Africa : Verses,* with the Executors of Mr. Kingsley

Fairbridge for "The Naming Song of Kusawa Afa" and other poems from *Selected Poems,* and for "Joys Seven" from *The Oxford Book of Carols*; Messrs. J. C. Juta (S. Africa) for poems by Beatrice M. Bromley : "Where the Aloe Grows" and "The Song of Table Bay"; Mr. Leonard Flemming for "The Wind at Dawn"; the Executors of Mr. Crosbie Garstin for "On the Back Veld" and "The Transport Rider"; Miss June Daly for "The Kraals" and "The Captive Lion"; Messrs. Blackwell & Co. for "Cape Town from Platte Klip," by E. Berlein; Mr. Francis Carey Slater for "Lines from 'Zambesi'" and other poems, with Messrs. Ernest Benn Ltd. for the lyrics from *Drought*, with Messrs. Blackwood & Sons for poems from *Dark Folk*; Mr. Charles Ould for "Red," "Voortrekkers" and "Green Waters"; Mr. C. C. Woollacott for "The Abandoned Mine"; Mrs. Olive R. Bridgman for "Three Ships" and "A Ballad of Weenen."

To Messrs. Sidgwick & Jackson Ltd. for "The Settlers" from *Mendicant Rhymes* and "The Song of the Builders" from *Little Plays of St. Francis,* by Laurence Housman, for "The Bridge," by J. R. Anderson from *Walls and Hedges* and for "I Sing of a Maiden" from *Early English Lyrics* chosen by E. K. Chambers and F. Sidgwick; the Rev. A. Vine Hall for "Thomas Pringle" from *Poems of a South African*; Messrs. Chatto & Windus for "The Far Farers," by R. L. Stevenson from *New Poems*; Messrs. Constable & Co. with the Executors of the late William Blane for "A Pioneer's Epitaph" from *A Ballad of Men and other Verses,* and with Mr. Gordon Bottomley for "The Ploughman"; the proprietors of *Punch* for "David Livingstone"; Messrs. Ivor Nicholson & Watson Ltd. with Denys Lefebvre for "The Voortrekker" and "Oom Paul" from *The Lone Trek*; the Executors of the late Andrew Lang for "Zimbabwe"; the Rev. Arthur Shearly Cripps for "A Rhyme of Chaminuka"; Messrs. Arnold & Co. with the Executrix for "An Inscription" from *Edmund Garrett : A Memoir,* by Sir E. T. Cook; Messrs. Methuen

& Co. with the Executrix of the late Rudyard Kipling for " The Burial " and " Sussex " from *The Five Nations*; the Executors of the late William A. Way for " The Shangani Memorial."

To Mrs. Harold Munro of the Poetry Bookshop for " On Youth Struck Down," by Charlotte Mew; Messrs. Philpott & Collins (Bulawayo) for " The Pace of the Ox," by Cullen Gouldsbury; Messrs. John Lane the Bodley Head Ltd. for " To the Springboks in England, 1932 " from *Mithraic Emblems,* by Roy Campbell; the Hogarth Press for " The Ecstatic " and " Sing we the Two Lieutenants " from *A Time to Dance* and " In these Our Winter Days " from *The Magnetic Mountain,* all by Cecil Day Lewis; Messrs. J. M. Dent & Sons with Mr. Herbert Palmer for " Woodworker's Ballad " from *Collected Poems* and " David and Goliath " from *The Gallows Cross*; Mr. Siegfried Sassoon for " The Mystic as Soldier " from *Selected Poems* (Wm. Heinemann Ltd.); Mr. Laurence Binyon for " Hunger "; Messrs. Martin Secker and Warburg Ltd. for " To a Poet a Thousand Years Hence," by J. E. Flecker, from *Collected Poems.*

" I Love all Beauteous Things " is taken from *The Shorter Poems of Robert Bridges* by permission of the Clarendon Press, Oxford; " On Malvern Hill " is reprinted from *Collected Poems of John Masefield* (Wm. Heinemann Ltd.) by permission of the author; and " The Signaller " and " Exile in August," by Arthur Shearly Cripps, are reprinted from *Lake and War* by permission of Messrs. Basil Blackwell & Mott Ltd., Oxford. Mr. Miller's poem, " Armistice Day, 1938," is from *South African Harvest.*

"Beat! Beat! Beat!"
Drum that dost set our feet
Stepping a-step with Spring!

ARTHUR SHEARLY CRIPPS.

1

A PSALM OF DAVID

O LORD our Lord, how excellent is thy name in all the
    earth,
Who hast set thy glory above the heavens !

Out of the mouth of babes and sucklings hast thou ordained
    strength because of thine enemies,
That thou mightest still the enemy and the avenger.

When I consider thy heavens, the work of thy fingers,
The moon and the stars, which thou hast ordained ;

What is man, that thou art mindful of him ?
And the son of man, that thou visitest him ?

For thou hast made him a little lower than the angels,
And hast crowned him with glory and honour.

Thou madest him to have dominion over the works of thy
    hands ;
Thou hast put all things under his feet :

All sheep and oxen,
Yea, and the beasts of the field ;

The fowl of the air, and the fish of the sea,
And whatsoever passeth through the paths of the seas.

O Lord our Lord, how excellent is thy name in all the
    earth !
                                        Psalm viii.

I LOVE ALL BEAUTEOUS THINGS

I LOVE all beauteous things,
I seek and adore them ;
God hath no better praise,
And man in his hasty days
Is honoured for them.

I too will something make
And joy in the making ;
Altho' to-morrow it seem
Like the empty words of a dream
Remembered on waking.

Robert Bridges.

3

THUNDERSTORMS

MY mind has thunderstorms,
That brood for heavy hours ;
Until they rain me words,
My thoughts are drooping flowers
And sulking, silent birds.

Yet come, dark thunderstorms,
And brood your heavy hours ;
For when you rain me words
My thoughts are dancing flowers
And joyful singing birds.

W. H. Davies.

4

SHELLEY'S SKYLARK

(The neighbourhood of Leghorn: March, 1887)

SOMEWHERE afield here something lies
In Earth's oblivious eyeless trust
That moved a poet to prophecies—
A pinch of unseen, unguarded dust :

The dust of the lark that Shelley heard,
And made immortal through times to be;—
Though it only lived like another bird,
And knew not its immortality :

Lived its meek life; then, one day, fell—
A little ball of feather and bone;
And how it perished, when piped farewell,
And where it wastes, are alike unknown.

Maybe it rests in the loam I view,
Maybe it throbs in a myrtle's green,
Maybe it sleeps in the coming hue
Of a grape on the slopes of yon inland scene.

Go find it, faeries, go and find
That tiny pinch of priceless dust,
And bring a casket silver-lined,
And framed of gold that gems encrust;

And we will lay it safe therein,
And consecrate it to endless time;
For it inspired a bard to win
Ecstatic heights in thought and rhyme.

Thomas Hardy.

THE FOREST BIRD

THE loveliest things of earth are not
   Her lilies, waterfalls, or trees;
Or clouds that float like still, white stones
   Carved upon azure seas;
 Or snow-white orchids, scarlet-lipped
   In darkness of damp woods,
   In hush of shadowy leaves;
Or the pale foam that lights the coast
   Of earth on moonless eves.

The moon is lovely, and the sea's
   Bright shadow on the sand;
The phantom vessel as it glides
   Out from a phantom land;
And, hung above the shadowed earth,
   Moored in a crystal sky,
   That fleet of phantom lights:
These are but Beauty's fading flags,
   Her perishable delights.

But in transparency of thought
   Out of the branched, dark-foliaged word
There flits a strange, soft-glimmering light,
   Shy as a forest bird.
Most lovely and most shy it comes
   From realm of sense unknown,
   And sings of earthly doom,
Of an immortal happiness
   In the soul's deepening gloom.

W. J. Turner.

TO A PET COBRA

WITH breath indrawn and every nerve alert,
As at the brink of some profound abyss,
I love on my bare arm, capricious flirt,
To feel the chilly and incisive kiss
Of your lithe tongue that forks its swift caress
Between the folded slumber of your fangs,
And half reveals the nacreous recess
Where death upon those dainty hinges hangs.

Our lonely lives in every chance agreeing,
It is no common friendship that you bring.
It was the desert starved us into being,
The hate of men that sharpened us to sting;
Sired by starvation, suckled by neglect,
Hate was the surly tutor of our youth:
I too can hiss the hair of men erect
Because my lips are venomous with truth.

Where the hard rock is barren, scorched the spring,
Shrivelled the grass, and the hot wind of death
Hornets the crag with whirred metallic wing—
We drew the fatal secret of our breath:
By whirlwinds bugled forth, whose funnelled suction
Scrolls the spun sand into a golden spire,
Our spirits leaped, hosannas of destruction,
Like desert lilies forked with tongues of fire.

Dainty one, deadly one, whose folds are panthered
With stars, my slender Kalahari flower,
Whose lips with fangs are delicately anthered,
Whose coils are volted with electric power,

I love to think how men of my dull nation
Might spurn your sleep with inadvertent heel
To kindle up the lithe retaliation
And caper to the slash of sudden steel.

There is no sea so wide, no waste so steril
But holds a rapture for the sons of strife:
There shines upon the topmost peak of peril
A throne for spirits that abound in life:
There is no joy like theirs who fight alone,
Whom lust or gluttony have never tied,
Who in their purity have built a throne,
And in their solitude a tower of pride.

I wish my life, O suave and silent sphinx,
Might flow like yours in some such strenuous line,
My days the scales, my years the bony links
That chain the length of its resilient spine:
And when at last the moment comes to strike,
Such venom give my hilted fangs the power,
Like drilling roots the dirty soil that spike,
To sting these rotted wastes into a flower.

Roy Campbell.

7

THE SCRIBE

WHAT lovely things
   Thy hand hath made:
The smooth-plumed bird
   In its emerald shade,
The seed of the grass,
   The speck of stone
Which the wayfaring ant
   Stirs—and hastes on !

26

Though I should sit
  By some tarn in thy hills,
Using its ink
  As the spirit wills
To write of Earth's wonders,
  Its live, willed things,
Flit would the ages
  On soundless wings
Ere unto Z
  My pen drew nigh;
Leviathan told,
  And the honey-fly:

And still would remain
  My wit to try—
My worn reeds broken,
  The dark tarn dry,
All words forgotten—
  Thou, Lord, and I.

Walter de la Mare.

8

THE POETS

ANY honest housewife would sort them out,
Having a nose for fish, an eye for apples.
Is it any mystery who are the sound,
And who the rotten ?   Never, by her lights.

Any honest housewife who, by ill-fortune,
Ever engaged a slut to scrub for her
Could instantly distinguish from the workers
The lazy, the liars and the petty thieves.

Does this denote a sixth peculiar sense
Gifted to housewives for their vestal needs ?
Or is it a failure of the usual five
In all unthrifty writers on this head ?

Robert Graves.

9

WINTER THE HUNTSMAN

THROUGH his iron glades
Rides Winter the Huntsman.
All colour fades
As his horn is heard sighing.

Far through the forest
His wild hooves crash and thunder
Till many a mighty branch
Is torn asunder.

And the red reynard creeps
To his hole near the river,
The copper leaves fall
And the bare trees shiver

As night creeps from the ground,
Hides each tree from its brother,
And each dying sound
Reveals yet another.

Is it Winter the Huntsman
Who gallops through his iron glades,
Cracking his cruel whip
To the gathering shades ?

Osbert Sitwell.

10

TWELFTH NIGHT

Windy with January gold,
　　Day waned o'er Arven's towers;
The North Wind's breath serene and cold
　　Scattered the sunset flowers.

Each street-end showed in a dying flare
　　The young year's ecstasy;
All the waste spaces of the air
　　Boiled like a seething sea.

I saw the New Year like a Prince
　　In a coat of cloth of gold,
With feet of pearl and lips of quince,
　　Ride in from the bare wold.
　　　　　　　　Wilfrid Rowland Childe.

11

THE RAINBOW

I saw the lovely arch
Of Rainbow span the sky,
The gold sun burning
As the rain swept by.

In bright-ringed solitude
The showery foliage shone
One lovely moment,
And the Bow was gone.
　　　　　　　　Walter de la Mare.

THE SOLITARY REAPER

BEHOLD her, single in the field,
Yon solitary Highland Lass!
Reaping and singing by herself;
Stop here, or gently pass!
Alone she cuts and binds the grain,
And sings a melancholy strain;
O listen! for the vale profound
Is overflowing with the sound.

No nightingale did ever chaunt
More welcome notes to weary bands
Of travellers in some shady haunt,
Among Arabian sands:
A voice so thrilling ne'er was heard
In spring-time from the cuckoo-bird
Breaking the silence of the seas
Among the farthest Hebrides.

Will no one tell me what she sings?
Perhaps the plaintive numbers flow
For old, unhappy, far-off things,
And battles long ago:
Or is it some more humble lay,
Familiar matter of to-day?
Some natural sorrow, loss, or pain,
That has been, and may be again?

Whate'er the theme, the maiden sang
As if her song could have no ending;
I saw her singing at her work,
And o'er the sickle bending; —
I listened, motionless and still;
And, as I mounted up the hill,

The music in my heart I bore,
Long after it was heard no more.
William Wordsworth.

13

PYLONS

OVER the tree'd upland evenly striding,
One after one they lift their serious shapes
That ring with light. The statement of their steel
Contradicts Nature's softer architecture.
Earth will not accept them as it accepts
A wall, a plough, a church so coloured of earth
It might be some experiment of the soil's.
Yet are they outposts of the trekking future.
Into the thatch-hung consciousness of hamlets
They blaze new thoughts, new habits.
                                        Traditions
Are being trod down like flowers dropped by children.
Already that farm-boy striding and throwing seed
In the shoulder-hinged half-circle Millet knew
Looks grey with antiquity as his dead forbears,
A half familiar figure out of the Georgics,
Unheeded by these new-world, rational towers.
                                Stanley Snaith.

14

THE LION

STRANGE spirit with inky hair,
    Tail tufted stiff in rage,
I saw with sudden stare
    Leap on the printed page.

The stillness of its roar
　　From midnight deserts torn
Clove silence to the core
　　Like the blare of a great horn.

I saw the sudden sky;
　　Cities in crumbling sand;
The stars fall wheeling by;
　　The lion roaring stand:

The stars fall wheeling by,
　　Their silent, silver stain,
Cold on his glittering eye,
　　Cold on his carven mane.

The full-orbed moon shone down,
　　The silence was so loud,
From jaws wide-open thrown
　　His voice hung like a cloud.

Earth shrank to blackest air,
　　That spirit stiff in rage
Into some midnight lair
　　Leapt from the printed page.

W. J. Turner.

15

INDIA

THEY hunt, the velvet tigers in the jungle,
The spotted jungle full of shapeless patches—
Sometimes they're leaves, sometimes they're hanging
　　flowers,
Sometimes they're hot gold patches of the sun:
They hunt, the velvet tigers in the jungle!

What do they hunt by glimmering pools of water,
By the round silver Moon, the pool of Heaven:
In the striped grass, amid the barkless trees—
The Stars scattered like eyes of beasts above them!

What do they hunt, their hot breath scorching insects,
Insects that blunder blindly in the way,
Vividly fluttering—they also are hunting,
Are glittering with a tiny ecstasy !

The grass is flaming and the trees are growing,
The very mud is gurgling in the pools,
Green toads are watching, crimson parrots flying,
Two pairs of eyes meet one another glowing—
They hunt, the velvet tigers in the jungle.

W. J. Turner.

16

BEAUTY THE PILGRIM

BEAUTY the Pilgrim
    Carries no purse;
He pays his needs
    With a snatch of verse;
He mends his coat,
    And cobbles his shoes,
With a song, with a dream, with a thread
    Of the world's good news.

Beauty the Pilgrim
    Came to my door;
But I was busy
    Counting my store;
And when I looked up
    Where day had shone,

My store was withered away
And Beauty gone.

Gerald Gould.

17

CHERRY TREES

LOVELIEST of trees, the cherry now
Is hung with bloom along the bough,
And stands about the woodland ride
Wearing white for Eastertide.

Now, of my threescore years and ten,
Twenty will not come again,
And take from seventy springs a score,
It only leaves me fifty more.

And since to look at things in bloom
Fifty springs are little room,
About the woodlands I will go
To see the cherry hung with snow.

A. E. Housman.

18

THE SUNSHINE LAND

BLUE skies burning above
  Leagues of brown earth and sand;
This is the land that we cherish and love,
  This is the Sunshine Land. . . .

Her silence sings to the soul:
  She beckons with unseen hand
When surly seas bellow and roll
  'Twixt us and her bright strand.

Unto this earth we own,
    Love, and serve while we live,
Our blood and bone for fountain and stone
    After life shall we give.

Blue skies burning above
    Leagues of brown earth and sand:
This is the land that we cherish and love,
    This is the Sunshine Land.

                                    Francis Carey Slater.

19

TO THE VELD

RAGGED brown carpet, vast and bare,
Seamed with grey rocks, scathed black with flame !
Stage-carpet, foil for all that's fair!
O'er thy grim stretches dance in air
Sun, moon and stars in dazzling wear—
Enhanced their splendour by thy shame.

Poor, unloved!   Take my love and praise—
Not most because so faery-fine
Heaven peeps at poverty of thine,
Nor because thy mute exile days
Teach best the worth of greenwood ways,
And meadows where deep waters shine!

Nay most of all for weariness—
The homeless void, the endless track,
Noon-thirst, and wintry night's distress—
For all tense stretchings on the rack—
That gave me my lost manhood back!

                                    Arthur Shearly Cripps.

20

AFAR IN THE DESERT

AFAR in the Desert I love to ride,
With the silent Bush-boy alone by my side:
O'er the brown Karroo, where the bleating cry
Of the springbok's fawn sounds plaintively;
And the timorous quagga's shrill whistling neigh
Is heard by the fountain at twilight grey;
Where the zebra wantonly tosses his mane,
With wild hoof scouring the desolate plain;
And the fleet-footed ostrich over the waste
Speeds like a horseman who travels in haste,
Hieing away to the home of her rest,
Where she and her mate have scooped their nest,
Far hid from the pitiless plunderer's view
In the pathless depths of the parched **Karroo.**

Afar in the Desert I love to ride,
With the silent Bush-boy alone by my side:
Away—away in the Wilderness vast,
Where the White Man's foot hath never passed,
And the quivered Koranna or Bechuan
Hath rarely crossed with his roving clan:
A region of emptiness, howling and drear,
Which Man hath abandoned from famine and fear;
Which the snake and the lizard inhabit alone,
With the twilight bat from the yawning stone;
Where grass, nor herb, nor shrub takes root,
Save poisonous thorns that pierce the foot;
And the bitter-melon for food and drink
Is the pilgrim's fare by the salt-lake's brink:
A region of drought, where no river glides,
Nor rippling brook with osiered sides;
Where sedgy pool, nor bubbling fount,
Nor tree, **nor** cloud, nor misty mound

Appears, to refresh the aching eye:
But the barren earth and the burning sky,
And the black horizon, round and round,
Spread—void of living sight or sound.

From " Afar in the Desert,"
Thomas Pringle.

21

CAMP FIRE

RED of the bushwood fire,
Blue smoke-film drifting high,
Sombrely gaunt and still
Brown tents against the sky—
Soft stir of yoke-freed beasts
Wandering near at hand,
Secret-whispering wind
Ruffling the sunburnt sand.

Out of the growing dusk—
Cry of a distant herd,
Crack of a far-off whip,
Plaint of a lonely bird,
Sinking glow of the fire,
Ashen veiling of light—
Dream-winged, tenderly strange,
Over the veld broods Night.

Beatrice Marian Bromley.

22

THE WIND AT DAWN

THERE is a wind that very softly passes
Over the earth before the break of day,
Rustling the reeds and forest leaves and grasses,
Rippling the waters that so tranquil lay.

Over the plains and swiftly through the hollows,
Whispering lowly of the coming morn,
It passes with a trembling touch—then follows
The solemn silence that precedes the dawn.

It is a wind that coldly comes, and sighing,
For it has met and taken in its flight
The breath of those the sunset had left dying,
And all the souls that had been freed at night.
It is a wind that wakes a world all sleeping,
The sighing of a night that fades away,
And, with the night's dark secrets in its keeping,
Passes beyond—and heralds in the day.

Leonard Flemming.

23

DAY

DAY !
Faster and more fast,
O'er night's brim, day boils at last;
Boils, pure gold, o'er the cloud-cup's brim
Where spurting and supprest it lay—
For not a froth-lake touched the rim
Of yonder gap in the solid gray
Of the eastern cloud, an hour away;
But forth one wavelet, then another, curled,
Till the whole sunrise, not to be supprest,
Rose, reddened, and its seething breast
Flickered in bounds, grew gold, then overflowed the world.

From " Pippa Passes."

Robert Browning.

24

HOME WITH DAWN

MILE after mile, so many a mile—
The last mile left—I stride for home.
Cock in yon thatched hut, do you hear
My joyful tidings, as I come,
That "Hail! Hail! Hail!" you cry so clear?

Why wraps that golden, tender smile
The tired moon's face as down she goes?
She was so proud and stern and white—
When I was far, and high she rose:
Knows she that now my home's in sight?

Ah! While I come, the self-same while,
Even as I the door unlatch,
He comes—for whom the dead moon smiled—
Whom the cock cried for through the thatch—
Dawn, treading soft as tip-toe child,
Deigning each dusty window through
A dewy glimpse of gold and blue.

Arthur Shearly Cripps.

25

ON THE BACK VELD

THE red flame-flowers bloom and die,
The embers puff a golden spark,
Now and again a horse's eye
Shines like a topaz in the dark.

A distant jackal jars the hush,
The drowsy oxen champ and sigh,
The ghost moon peers above the bush
And creeps across the starry sky.

Low in the South the Cross is bright,
And sleep comes dreamless, undefiled,
Here in the blue and silver night,
In the Star-Chamber of the Wild.

Crosbie Garstin.

26

THE TRANSPORT RIDER

Old Zambesi Road

" M'PURRU " kicks the glowing logs,
And stirs about the blackened pot
Of steaming mealie pap; the dogs
Creep up lest they should be forgot.
" Five " twangs his fiddle gut and wails
His nightly dirge. With hissing breath,
Old " Klaas," the driver, spins his tales
Of lion hunts and sudden death.

The oxen slumber at their reims,
Each by his yoke a shadowy blot,
Grunting and wandering in their dreams
Through happy meads where droughts are not.
The million million stars are lit,
The sky is pricked with spark and gem;
They wink down at my fire and it
Respectfully winks back at them.

Crosbie Garstin.

27

SPRING

i. WAITING FOR THE RAINS

THE land is black with fires and bare
  Ere the warm rushing of the rains,
Yet blood-dipt leaf and bloom declare
  How sap runs high in forest veins.
Blue cup with sunrise-ruddied brink
Hast no drops yet for Earth to drink?

Copper and gold dance eastern trees,
  As pipes the wind and climbs the sun.
Hark! Leaden fall of oranges!
  See! Branch-flowers from moon-silver spun!
God, when wilt press within Thy cup
One wine-skin cloud for Earth to sup?

28

ii. AFTER RAINS

Where the fire scathed, the green grass grows,
  Our black bowls bring of milk no dearth,
The hard hearts of a hundred hoes
  Beat at the melted heart of Earth!
Their nightly lauds for drunkards' fill,
Cricket and frog sing hoarse and shrill.

New births are ripening in the womb;
  Our furrowed gardens, big with seed,
Grow jocund at the thunder-gloom,
  And lap and suck for mothers' need.
To hoe! To hoe! Ere mounts the sun!
The wine is poured, the feast begun!

Arthur Shearly Cripps.

29

THE KRAALS

GREY on the hill's grey side they lie,
Light-blanketed by sun and sky.
As much unhid, as oft unguessed,
As the shy grass-bird's shallow nest.

Grey on the hill's green side they dream
While goat-herds drowse by trampled stream,
And cattle, lowing as they graze,
Break the deep silence of the days.

June Daly.

30

CHARTER-COUNTRY

Charter District, Mashonaland

How shall I paint or how personify
Her land so manifold—
So simply lit, most days, with suns of gold,
So simply roofed, most days, with skies of blue ?
Praise we her plough-soils, praise her pastures fat!
Praise we her lack of mines (praise God for that!)

Paint her as Naiad—nymph of fount or spring
And many a river's urn—
Whence waters outpoured east or westward turn!
Sanyati and Ngezi, gathering
Sebakwe to them, own her motherhood:
She cradles Sabi's ocean-reaching flood.

Paint her as Oread—nymph of height and hill—
Throned on her granite grey!
Wedza's blue cones beyond her frontier stay,
But all a Titan-warfare's overspill
(Zwinjanja's cragland)'s hers.   She counts her own
Manizi's menace, Chinembeza's frown.

Paint her as Dryad—nymph of timeless trees
Strown far to south and east,
Dweller in wild sand orchards where we feast
On stony apples, tough-shelled oranges,
Wardress of rock-groves too, for charcoal good—
Clustering on ridge where some lost smithy stood!

How shall you paint and how personify
Her close-lipped quiet land?
How will you best her secrets understand ?
First learn to love and live with her as I,
Then leave for exile.   Ere you come again—
Trust her to make each wistful secret plain!

Arthur Shearly Cripps.

31

CAPE TOWN FROM PLATTE KLIP

Winter Evening

THEN in a pause between the day and dark
The world had slid into another space,
The Time we know had slipt its boundary,
And the dim city swayed into a dream.

Beyond the town a cold enchanted sea
Slept, tranced by visions of pale ships that sail
O'er desolate oceans white with moonshine,
Dream ships, dream ships, a dreaming spell-bound sea.

A sudden bell cleaves through the deepening dusk,
The immortal dream breaks into mortal flower
As the town's myriad lamps leap into life:
And the world's pieces are Time's toys again.

Only the mountain stands remote, withdrawn,
A cairn of darkness on the fading sky,
Then o'er the edge of darkness—magical
Flows the bright ripple of the waiting moon.

E. Berlein.

32

THE WAY IN AFRICA

(" What is that which has no End ? The Way."—*African
Riddle.*)

I SAID, " I'll go my road alone."
I rose while yet the dawn was gray,
And lo! beneath me and before
Companioned me the Way.

And while the East wore arras rich,
And when the sun came up and shone,
That comrade kept her secret close,
And lured me by it on.

Great golden vleis, and granite hills
So far and blue, she'd have me see,
But under foot her deep sand sighed,
" Better is yet to be."

And as I dined in thorn-tree shade,
And lipped a deep-bowled spruit for cup—
The Way, to me the way-worn, sighed
By dust-wisps—" On and up!"

Of rise and dip, and dip and rise,
And fence, with here and there a gate,
I wearied, but she wandered on—
Her hope insatiate.

Meseemed that—swerving at the drift
As eve grew dim—my track was lost:
Then up the hill the white Way rose
Before me like a ghost.

And still with signals on and on,
For many a darkling drouthy mile,
She flagged me white from hope to hope
In silence all that while.

What time the town's few lamps at last
Long my impatient feet defied—
I grew to loathe and love by turns
My pale and patient guide.

So 'mid the lamps at last we came,
We came together, she and I,
And I went in to sup and sleep
But she went wandering by.

Arthur Shearly Cripps.

33

ROUNDING THE CAPE

The low sun whitens on the flying squalls,
Against the cliffs the long grey surge is rolled
Where Adamastor from his marble halls
Threatens the sons of Lusus as of old.

Faint on the glare uptowers the dauntless form,
Into whose shade abysmal as we draw,
Down on our decks, from far above the storm,
Grin the stark ridges of his broken jaw.

Across his back, unheeded, we have broken
Whole forests: heedless of the blood we've spilled,
In thunder still his prophecies are spoken,
In silence, by the centuries, fulfilled.

Farewell, terrific shade! though I go free
Still of the powers of darkness art thou Lord:
I watch the phantom sinking in the sea
Of all that I have hated or adored.

The prow glides smoothly on through seas quiescent :
But where the last point sinks into the deep,
The land lies dark beneath the rising crescent,
And Night, the Negro, murmurs in his sleep.

Roy Campbell.

34

LINES FROM "ZAMBESI"

FORGOTTEN now the weariness of long leagues travelled;
Dust were past dreams and mist each travel-story;
The knotted skein of distance was unravelled,
I saw Zambesi in his magnitude and glory.
I saw the wild trees dance, the mad rocks leap
Against behemoth-heave and lightning-sweep
Of water down bewildered precipices
Into fiend-racked abysses.

And from the tumult of that hellish cauldron
Swift, silvery vapours rose,
Girded with iridescent bows,
To hail the harping sun.
Yes, then I saw Zambesi's leaping flocks,
Bearded Angora rams with sweeping locks,
Curled snow-white fleeces streaked with gold,
Ten million in a moment flashed,
Ten million in a moment crashed
To the rapacious fold.

Francis Carey Slater.

35

RED

Hibiscus was red,
(It grew by the window,)
And salvia,
Poinsettia,
The spikes of aloes,
And the Kaffir boom
In flaring splendour.

Here there are flowers,
Frail lives of loveliest name,
Daffodils, primroses, daisies,
Fritillaries, buttercups—
But nowhere in England
That pagan colour,
Nowhere that red
That flamed at the window.

Charles Ould.

FIVE LYRICS FROM "DROUGHT"

i

DAY on day of crashing sunlight,
When the hammer-blows of heat,
The intolerable dazzle,
Blaze and blare of the sun
Are like the stubborn braying,
The arrogant braying,
The soul-destructive braying
Of instruments of brass.

Forgotten, long forgotten
Are the shining melodies,
The violin-melodies
Of lightly falling rain;
Forgotten, long forgotten
Are the silvery ecstasies
Of softly flowing streams,
Of dream-entangled streams.

Shrill cornets screech,
Brazen saxophones blare,
Bray, blaze, and blare
Discordant jazz-tunes,
Soul-racking and hideous—
An interminable fugue
Of blaze, dazzle and glare;
An intolerable Te Deum
Of soulless and senseless Drought—
Implacable Drought.

ii

POWDER is the grass, burnt powder,
Mingled now with the dust from which it sprung;
Dead are the lilies in the veld-pans;
The veld-flowers have vanished.

Naked is the veld, scorched and naked,
Charred is its coat, once brave and green;
Naked to the sun's lash it quivers—
A victim defenceless.

Silent are the streams, sad and silent;
Drought has sucked their shining souls away;
The stars have slipped from their fingers,
The moon has escaped them.

Dead are the blossoms and the berries,
The bright birds have departed,
Like poor-whites, they have fluttered to the cities,
And there they starve songless.

Dead are the friendly sheep and cattle:
Bleached bones whiten in the sun;
No soft lowing comes from the valleys,
No faint bleat from the hills.

Lonely is the veld, stark and lonely,
On its scarred breast no living thing is seen,
Save only a hawk that hovers,
Like doom o'er its shadow.

Drought—the dark vulture—hovers,
Desolation—his shadow—swings below,
Over the long-drawn anguish
And despair of the veld.

38

iii

SOFTLY and quietly across the waiting mountains,
Softly and quietly and while we slept in sorrow,
Sure of its way even in the heart of darkness,
Came the redeeming rain:
Came even as sleep to strained and weary eyeballs,
Came even as rest to toil-racked limbs and tired,
Came even as love to souls in desolation,
So came the rain.

Softly and quietly across stone-crested mountains,
Over scarred plains, stark moors and herbless valleys,
Finding sure pathways through the woods of darkness,
Came the redeeming rain:
Came in the night and drummed upon the housetops,
Came in the night and whispered at our windows.
We who had slept in sorrow woke in gladness,
Called by the rain.

39

iv

SUDDENLY the drums of the rain are beating,
Over the hills her shining banner comes;
Swiftly the enemy drought is retreating—
Scared by insistent drums.
Painfully and long has the veld been battered,
Smitten and scourged by devils of drought,—
Sweepingly the stubborn foe is shattered,
Rain has put him to rout.
Suddenly comes rain with his shining legions,
(Will love come so, bringing peace to earth?)
Suddenly long blasted and barren regions
Wake to the wonder of birth.

V

ONCE more the kingfisher
Admires the gleam
Of his rainbow-reflection
In the gay stream;
The crow, sooty-coated,
With never a pause
Scratches up the sown mealies
And raspily caws;
The dazzling sunbird,
Wee flower-like fellow,
Sips honey from blossoms
To make his voice mellow;
And the wild green canary,
Without stay or stop,
Drops shining song-bubbles
From the treetop.

Francis Carey Slater.

41

SUMMER RAIN-SONG

WIDELY spread your wings of dun-grey woof
O'er our tilths, O rain,
Bill and coo and chuckle on my roof
All a night again!
Brood and scatter silver-fluttering sheen
O'er our valley's nest, and round its arching brink—
Till the brown seeds hatch, the tender new-fledged green
Tongue by tongue, leap forth to drink!

Arthur Shearly Cripps.

THE ABANDONED MINE

A HEAP of rock marks the abandoned mine ;
The veld's unpitying silence lies around
Those broken stones—a mute and mournful sign
Of human enterprise with failure crowned.
Here is the trail along which used to pass
The workers to and fro: a narrow track
That winds away among the bush and grass—
But those who trod it will no more come back!
Time, with slow hands, shall form the scene anew,
Repair the gashes in the wounded soil,
And cover up the last remaining clue
To a poor useless record of men's toil.
And this, the mound they built when hopes were high,
Shall be a grave where those hopes buried lie.

C. C. Woollacott.

43

THE BUSHMEN

TAMELESS and fierce and foul were these pygmies, and cun-
    ning as serpents;
  Callous spawn of the desert, dull to the sting of its sun.
Hunted, with pitiless hate, they crouched among sheltering
    koppies;
  Tortured with famine and thirst, they crawled through
    the scrub after prey.
Lurking in hidden places—dark crevices, gloom-haunted
    caverns—
  Limned they on rock and on boulder lasting signs of their
    art;
Brutish were they and unclean, yet—stirred by some glim-
    mer of beauty—
  Thirsted to capture in colour the life of a vanishing dream!

Dust are those fugitive pygmies, blown by the winds of
    the desert,
  Crushed and heedlessly trodden 'neath heels of hurrying
    change;
Hunters and haters of men, their hatred has crumbled to
    ashes;
  Hated of men and hunted, hatred pursues them no more.
Clumsy weapons of stone, rough bows and a handful of
    arrows—
  Relics of hunger and hate—only remain of their lives;
But looming from cave and krans are inscribed in colours
    that fade not
  Hints from the heart of their secret, symbols and signs
    of their dreams.

From " The Karroo,"
Francis Carey Slater.

44

SONG OF THE WILD BUSHMAN

Let the proud White Man boast his flocks
    And fields of foodful grain;
My home is 'mid the mountain rocks,
    The Desert my domain.
I plant no herbs nor pleasant fruits,
    I toil not for my cheer;
The Desert yields me juicy roots
    And herds of bounding deer.

The countless springboks are my flock,
    Spread o'er the unbounded plain;
The buffalo bendeth to my yoke,
    The wild-horse to my rein;
My yoke is the quivering assegai,
    My rein the tough bow-string;
My bridle curb is a slender barb—
    Yet it quells the forest-king.

The crested adder honoureth me,
    And yields at my command
His poison-bag, like the honey-bee,
    When I seize him on the sand.
Yea, even the wasting locust-swarm,
    Which mighty nations dread,
To me nor terror brings nor harm—
    For I make of them my bread.

Thus I am lord of the Desert Land,
    And I will not leave my bounds
To crouch beneath the Christian's hand
    And kennel with his hounds:
To be a hound, and watch the flocks,
    For the cruel White Man's gain—
No! the brown Serpent of the Rocks
    His den doth yet retain;
And none who there his sting provokes
    Shall find its poison vain!

                        Thomas Pringle.

45

" VUKA "

(Xosa Morning Song)

THE red bull-sun is blazing on the mountains;
He stretches his burning bulk upon the rock-horned
    mountains;
He stamps and snorts, and from his flaming nostrils
Red-bellied mists escape and rise.
The red bull-sun is drinking at the fountains,
Fiercely he nuzzles the white-flanked fountains;
The sleeping fountains wake, and flying, flame and shiver,
Dazzled by his blazing eyes.

Wake, thou shining one, dark brown maiden;
Dazzle the sun's eyes, my heifer, shine!
Shine in my eyes, as in my soul thou shinest,
Wake, oh, wake, Lindani mine!

Francis Carey Slater.

46

LAMENT FOR A DEAD COW

(Chant by Xosa family on the death of Wetu, their only
cow)

SIYALILA, siyalila, inkomo yetu ifile! [1]
Beautiful was Wetu as a blue shadow
That nests on the grey rocks
About a sunbaked hilltop:
Her coat was black and shiny
Like an isipingo-berry;
Her horns were as sharp as the horns of the new moon
That tosses aloft the evening star;
Her round eyes were as clear and soft
As a mountain-pool
Where shadows dive from the high rocks.

No more will Wetu banish teasing flies
With her whistling tail;
No more will she face yapping curs
With lowered horns and bewildered eyes;
No more will her slow shadow
Comfort the sunburnt veld, and her sweet lowing
Delight the hills in the evening.
The fountain that filled our calabashes
Has been drained by a thirsty sun;

[1] We weep, we weep; our cow is dead!

The black cloud that brought us white rain
Has vanished—the sky is empty;
Our kraal is desolate;
Our calabashes are dry:
And we weep.

Francis Carey Slater.

47

NAMING SONG OF KUSAWA AFA

SHLANZA! Shlanza!
Thus was I named, Inkoos.
" Shlanza," they shouted, the men of Matshanga.
Swift rose my mother and fled to the reed-door—
Tore at the reeds, and behold! she was slaughtered—
Swiftly she died
And they shouted with laughter.

Then rose my father,
Grey Guru, my father,
And stumbled, wide-eyed, in the time of his waking;
Yea, stumbled and swore.
But the corpse of my mother lay still by the doorway,
And the blood of my mother was staining the lintel.

Then shouted grey Guru, old Guru, my father:
" You dogs of Matshanga!
You slay not grey Guru-
He dies by his hand! "
He tore at the thatch: with a brand from the fire
He kindled the roofing, and thick were the smoke-wreaths.
But over the shouting,
The shrieks of the slaughtered,
The cries of the women,
The songs of the slayers,

Makumbo Rashumba, who waited without,
Heard Guru; and thundered,
" Wait, filth, for thy slaying! "
And broke the wood-door with the blows of his kerrie.
I saw the hide shield and the head of the Tshangaan—
White were the plumes of the ostrich that decked it.
Makumbo Rashumba came cursing and choking;
For thick was the smoke, and the whirl of the fire
Licked red at the plumes on the head of the Slit-ear.

But Guru was dead.
In the flare of the fire
I saw the red blood on the throat of my father.
I screamed in my horror, and hurled at the Tshangaan
A beer-pot that lay on the ridge of the clay-shelf.
Makumbo Rashumba loud-laughed as he seized me:
" W'nasawa kuafa, heh ? Mwana ka Swina! "
And dragged me outside. And the flare of the village
Went red to the sky, and the flame of the village
Glared white on the timber, and white in the darkness
The smoke of the kaias whirled out on the night-wind,
And huddled together the women were moaning ;
The cattle were lowing with fear of the fires
And fear of the shouting, and groans of the dying,
And hot was the reek of the dead who were assegaied.
(Thickly they lay in the light of the fires!)

And down at the dance-ground the huts of Majaha
Were burning; and out on the dance-ground the Slit-ears
Had dragged the big war-drums and the best of the maidens.
And, beating the war-drums, the youth of the impi
Were starting a dance and a chant of Matshanga;
And seeing Rashumba they shouted with laughter—
For 'Kumbo Rashumba was greatest among them—
(A man of great strength, with the voice of a lion)
" Kazi feni! " they shouted, " Makumbo Makuru!

Rashumba ya ishla imwana ka Swina!"
But 'Kumbo Rashumba said: "Weary of women,
I live for the blood-smell; and now for my hunting
I take me a boy from the kraal of the Swina—
A boy who is frightened to die by the kerrie.
A boy who will cook for Makumbo Rashumba."

And thus was I named
By the men of Matshanga,
Who called me Kusawa—
Kusawa the Frightened.
But out of the dust and the blood of their hunting
I came on the soul of my father, grey Guru,
And learnt at the hand of Makumbo Rashumba,
Till I was a captain—
As brave as the bravest—
And ravaged Manika and slew the Maswina,
And looted Makoni—a land full of women—
Till out of the South, in the strength of their rifles,
The White Men advanced, and their peace was established.

                                        Kingsley Fairbridge.

48

THE SERF

His naked skin clothed in the torrid mist
That puffs in smoke around the patient hooves,
The ploughman drives, a slow somnambulist,
And through the green his crimson furrow grooves.
His heart, more deeply than he wounds the plain,
Long by the rasping share of insult torn,
Red clod, to which the war-cry once was rain
And tribal spears the fatal sheaves of corn,
Lies fallow now. But as the turf divides
I see in the slow progress of his strides

Over the toppled clods and falling flowers,
The timeless, surly patience of the serf
That moves the nearest to the naked earth
And ploughs down palaces, and thrones, and towers.

Roy Campbell.

49

THE SONG-MAKER

Alone in the hot sun,
On the hot sand in the sun,
Alone at the edge of the kraal,
In the dust of the dance-ground
Near the raised tobacco patch—
The women have gone to the fields,
The children have gone to play,
And the blind Maker of Songs
Sits here, alone, all day.

The dogs sniffed him and went.
The kraal-rats peer and go,
So very still he sits
Day long, and moon to moon,
His hands slack on the sand—
And he was just the same,
This maker of tribal songs,
Before the White Men came.

His was the song that woke
The war that brought their power;
The impi went with song—
Came back with song by night,
So many years ago,
With plunder every one;
Leaving among the dead,
Ganero, his only son.

And here, all day, he sits,
On the hot sand in the sun;
The children wonder if he sleeps,
And the flies think him dead,
The dogs smell him and go—
But to him is bare the lore
Of the Threshing and the Dancing Songs,
And the Chant that leads to War.

Kingsley Fairbridge.

50

XOSA SERENADE

ALL things lie hushed and quiet,
  Couched in the kraal of sleep,
Save the winds, that like cattle astray,
  Through the forest restlessly creep;
Save the moon, that antelope white,
  That steals through the clouds on high,
That wanders with silent footsteps
  Through the blossoming woods of the sky.
And like those winds I am restless—
  And ever on toward thee
My thoughts, with noiseless footsteps,
  Wander, O Zenani!

Francis Carey Slater.

51

THE ZULU GIRL

WHEN in the sun the hot red acres smoulder,
Down where the sweating gang its labour plies,
A girl flings down her hoe, and from her shoulder
Unslings her child tormented by the flies.

She takes him to a ring of shadow pooled
By thorn-trees: purpled with the blood of ticks,
While her sharp nails, in slow caresses ruled,
Prowl through his hair with sharp electric clicks,

His sleepy mouth, plugged by the heavy nipple,
Tugs like a puppy, grunting as he feeds:
Through his frail nerves her own deep languors ripple
Like a broad river sighing through its reeds.

Yet in that drowsy stream his flesh imbibes
An old unquenched unsmotherable heat—
The curbed ferocity of beaten tribes,
The sullen dignity of their defeat.

Her body looms above him like a hill
Within whose shade a village lies at rest,
Or the first cloud so terrible and still
That bears the coming harvest in its breast.

Roy Campbell.

52

GOD'S OWN COUNTRY

(Rural Africa)

CRYING as babes cry—
Her bronze-coloured Cherubim
Rap on their cheeks, and shrill—
" How long ?   How long, O Lord ? "
Thudding on hide-drums
Thunder her Seraphim—
Flapping their flight-wings
Of russet-brown feathers,
And roaring their drummers' tune—
" Africa!   Africa! "

High over Africa
Christ the Omnipotent
Shouts, and His " Thither! " brings
Stars from their sapphire lairs,
And shakes them in clusters down—
Silver and ruddy-gold—
To dance o'er her thatched huts
(Peaked huts of her poor men)
The steps His own Star danced—
That night the Kings came.

High stand those huts of hers,
Spearing the skyline,
Huts where her folk now—
Toil over—are sleeping;
While Africa, mother fond,
Bearing night-burdens theirs
Under the lighted sky,
Keeps watch o'er their cornlands—
Babe strapped in her goat-skin—
Full-bosomed—a Queen.

Hushed are all Angels now—
Watching o'er Africa:
Dim grows the smoke-cloud
O'er Africa's camp-fire:
Pale glows the crimson,
The gold in its brands' core:
Tawny and black-maned
The cloak wrapt about her—
She, hand-clapping meekly,
Gives ear to her Lord.

" *Blest are the wantless :*
Blessèd is Africa

(*Trudging her hill-paths*
From sun-up to sundown,
Gnawing her corn-cobs,
And munching her ground-nuts,
And cupping her wan palms
To quaff from her hill brooks) :
For I, King of Heaven,
Have crowned her My Queen.

" *Blest be her misery!*
Blessèd is Africa
(*Africa landless left,*
Homeless in home of hers,
Sucking on suff'rance grim
Dugs of her own earth) :
Caste-banned and colour-barred—
She smiles thro' her prison-fence—
Pressed down, running over—
Her comfort, her joy."

Hark!   Praise-Name on Praise-Name
Africa murmurs:
Pale palm laid on pale palm—
She claps in solemnity:
Hark! her gorges are screaming
Her Lord's loud Evangel:
Crag and cave, they have cried it,
Till dropt are their voices,
And in whispering bush-veld
The last echo dies.

Then Africa blows red
Her ashen-grey embers,
And wrapping her Lion-Skin
In loose folds about her,
To sleep lays her down.

Soon she dreams as a girl dreams
(In the watch of the morn-star—
One hour ere the cocks crow,)
Of her King, and her King's Queen,
Her comfort, her joy.

Arthur Shearly Cripps.

53

CLAY CATTLE

ONCE on a day of sun in the deep-grooved vale of the Tyumie,
River that draws its milk from the breast of the blue Amatola,
Riding along towards Hogsback I saw, close by the roadside,
Laughing, and flashing white teeth, a sprinkle of Xosa herdboys.
Cast aside were their clouts, their tattered blankets of sheepskin,
Naked they squatted, and shaped in clay, moist, pliable, yellow,
Oxen to plough the fields, sinewy, long-horned oxen;
Big-uddered cows to fill the round-bellied, red calabashes;
Sturdy, humpbacked bulls, and heifers with silken haunches.
Naked they sat in the sun, those pigmy gods and creators,
Moulding from worthless mud the coveted wealth of the Xosa—
Cattle to dapple the plains and loom like rocks on the hillside,
Cattle whose sweet soft lowing gladdens the hills in the evening:
Laughing they sat in the sun, those gay bronze-coloured herdboys,
Shaping in dull, dead earth their dreams of riches and beauty.

Haply, while moulding the mimic, their real kine had
  escaped them,
Haply, unheeded, their herds had strayed into fields of
  mealies;
Repentance would come with night when an irate father
  would greet them,
Stinging their shrinking rumps with strokes of his well-
  known 'swazi [1]
'Swazi that bites like a bug and stings like an angry hornet.
—Laughing they sat in the sun, those light-hearted, heedless
  herdboys,
Moulding in dull brown earth their dreams of beckoning
  beauty.

Francis Carey Slater.

54

BURIAL

(Among the Manyika a dead infant is buried by its mother
without a ceremony.)

YOWE, yowe, mwanango duku!
I bury you here by the edge of the lands.
Under the scrub and the weeds I bury you,
Here in the clay where the bracken grows.
Here on the hill the wind blows cold,
And the creepers are wet with the driving mist.
The grain-huts stand like ghosts in the mist,
And the water drips from their sodden thatch,
And the raindrops drip in the forest yonder
When the hill-wind shakes the heavy boughs.
Alas!   I am old, and you are the last—
Mwanango, the last of me, here on the hillside.

[1] Switch.

The dust where you played by the edge of the kraal
Is sodden with rain, and is trodden to mud.
The hoe that I use to fashion your dwelling
Is caked with the earth that is taking you from me.
Where now is Dzua who ripes the rukweza ?
And where now are you, O mwanango kaduku ?
Alas! Alas! My little child!
I bury you here by the edge of the lands.

Kingsley Fairbridge.

55

MANZI

Lately Manzi herded kine,
   Near the Amatola hills,
Slaked his thirst on crystal wine
   Bubbling from the mountain rills;
Sometimes he, with eager lip,
From stiff udders stole a sip—
Or, with guilty glance and laugh,
Snatched a ride upon a calf.

Manzi—who is hunter keen
   As ever stalked the mountain slope—
With his greyhound swift and lean
   Chased the nimble antelope—
Hurled his kerrie with true aim
At all birds that near him came.
If a sly snake raised its head—
Manzi smote, and it was dead!

When the day approached its noon,
   To the woods he would retire;
There he kindled, bright and soon,
   A jolly little hunter's fire,

Roasted near the ruddy blaze
Stripped and shining cobs of maize,
Or some bird of plumage bright
Which he crunched with quick delight.

Through the woods he then would stalk—
    Furtive as a nibbling mouse,
Keen-eyed as a hovering hawk,
    Still as lory 'mongst the boughs—
Liming twigs or setting snares
For unwary doves and hares,
Rifling the rich treasuries
Of the thrifty honey-bees.

Thus, untutored and untamed,
    Manzi walked the woods and hills
Careless, naked, unashamed,
    Joyous as the racing rills,
Laved his limbs in Tyumie's stream,
Dried them in the sunny beam,
Rolled upon the grass in play
Happy as the new-born day.

When the sun serenely stepped
    To his kraal in the far west,
And the snake-like shadows crept
    Stealthily from hidden nest,
Manzi drove his cattle home,
For the milking time was come,
Whistling as he went along
Or chanting some strange wordless song.

Milking o'er, in his kaross,
    Manzi, sitting near the blaze
Of wood-fed fires, drank amoss,
    And masticated golden maize—

Filled his greedy little tum
Tight as any battle drum—
And when stars began to peep
Manzi's stars were quenched in sleep.

Francis Carey Slater.

56

UMFETI

HERE, where the gnona bask
  But fifty yards away,
Under a withered palm
  Where children never play—
Sacred to him alone
  This strip of baking land—
'Feti, the Witch Doctor,
  Sits on the sand.

Here where the lizards climb
  Over his shrunken limbs,
Kindly the great sun shines,
  Kindly the great sun dims
Thoughts of the sombre past,
  Thoughts of the horrors done;
'Feti, the Witch Doctor,
  Nods in the sun.

High in the depthless blue
  The circling vultures wheel,
Over the burning sand
  Their silent shadows steal,
Over the aged man
  Silent a shadow flits;
'Feti, the Witch Doctor,
  Sleeps where he sits.

Down to the river's brink
  Go girls to fetch water,
Stop they at sight of him
  The father of slaughter,
Stop with averted eyes,
  Tremble and curtsey deep:
Tremble at sight of him
  Sitting asleep.

He is the touch of death,
  He is the feared of all,
Chiefs shake at sight of him,
  And the warriors tall
Shuffle uneasily—
  Fearing the eyes that pierce,
Fearing the Witch Doctor,
  'Feti the fierce.

From " Umfeti, the Witch Doctor,"
Kingsley Fairbridge.

57

AFRICAN WITCHCRAFT

(In time of Christmas)

COME, Hero-Child of Mary Queen,
Chase horrors hence in headlong rout!
Lantern (no evil wind blows out),
Keep watch at Yule our homes about!
Christ, wash our New Year white and clean,
By sovran spells of light and sheen,
From blight of malice, that unseen
Lies lurking in the dark without!

An ancient Oracle—Thy foe—
On Holy Night was speechless found:
That Night from Delphi's cloven ground
No fume arose; no dream-trance bound
Apollo's prophetess; her glow
Had failed her all that Night of snow—
That Night the Cock would sleepless crow—
That Night the Serpent slumbered sound.

Once more a witch-curst world amend,
Deliverer, born of Mary dear!
Pity a people dogged by fear
All days, all nights—from year to year!
Thou know'st the truth—what ghosts befriend
Women, what monsters men attend,
What fiends afflict and rage and rend.
Hell's harrower, all nights be near!

Arthur Shearly Cripps.

58

ASCRIPTION

IF aught of worth be in my psalms,
It in the Black Christ's Hands I lay,
In those Nail-grooved, hoe-hardened Palms
He holds to me now every day—
The Black Christ in Whose Name I pray,
Yet Who (O wonder!) prays to me
In wrong and need and contumely.

If any gift-of-sight of mine
Our land's veiled beauty should reveal,
My reader, to those eyes of thine,
That gift to Him Who gave assign!

To Him (Whose Feet unsandalled steal
Over the granite tracks I tread)
Head-haloed by our rose and gray
Of twilights, or our gold of day;
Who, near my red camp-fire, will spread
His reed-mat, or on rain-blessed days
Hoe deep His Pattern-work of praise
Full in my sight!

O happy eyes
Are mine that pierce the black disguise,
And see our Lord!   O woe of woe
That I should see, that I should know
Whom 'tis they use—that use Him so!

Arthur Shearly Cripps.

59

OUT OF THE ARK

Out of the Ark's grim hold
A torrent of splendour rolled—
From the hollow resounding sides,
Flashing and glittering, came
Panthers with sparkled hides,
And tigers scribbled with flame,
And lions in grisly trains
Cascading their golden manes.
They ramped in the morning light,
And over their stripes and stars
The sun-shot lightnings, quivering bright,
Rippled in zig-zag bars.
The wildebeest frisked with the gale
On the crags of a hunchback mountain,

With his heels in the clouds, he flirted his tail
Like the jet of a silvery fountain.
Frail oribi sailed with their golden-skinned
And feathery limbs laid light on the wind.
And the springbok bounded, and fluttered, and flew,
Hooping their spines on the gaunt karroo.
Grey zebras pranced and snorted aloud—
With the crackle of hail their hard hoofs pelt,
And thunder breaks from the rolling cloud
That they raise on the dusty Veld.
O, hark how the rapids of the Congo
Are chanting their rolling strains,
And the sun-dappled herds a-skipping to the song, go
Kicking up the dust on the great, grey plains—
Tsessebe, Koodoo, Buffalo, Bongo,
With the fierce wind foaming in their manes.

From " The Flaming Terrapin,"

Roy Campbell.

60

SPRINGBOKS

In the dawn-light blue they scatter the dew
From their flanks as they gambol on the grey Karroo.

They feed and stray; take fright—flash away—
And the pack that follows is a dun dust-spray:

Half buck, half bird! the veld is stirred
With the flashing ripple of that racing herd!

As dolphins play, hooping irised spray,
These curved, leaping racers loop air with clay;

Footballers, they shun their shadows and run
Heading-and-heeling at the red, round sun:

Brown breakers, they curl and their white manes hurl
At a beach—none may reach—the horizon's pearl.

From " The Trek,"
Francis Carey Slater.

61

A REBUKE TO THE PROUD

GAVEST thou the goodly wings unto the peacocks ?
Or wings and feathers unto the ostrich

Which leaveth her eggs in the earth,
And warmeth them in dust,

And forgetteth that the foot may crush them,
Or that the wild beast may break them ?

She is hardened against her young ones, as though they were
   not hers:
Her labour is in vain without fear;

Because God hath deprived her of wisdom,
Neither hath he imparted to her understanding.

What time she lifteth up herself on high,
She scorneth the horse and his rider.

Hast thou given the horse strength ?
Hast thou clothed his neck with thunder ?

Canst thou make him afraid as a grasshopper ?
The glory of his nostrils is terrible.

He paweth in the valley, and rejoiceth in his strength ;
He goeth on to meet the armed men.

He mocketh at fear, and is not affrighted;
Neither turneth he back from the sword.

The quiver rattleth against him,
The glittering spear and the shield.

He swalloweth the ground with fierceness and rage:
Neither believeth he that it is the sound of the trumpet.

He saith among the trumpets, Ha, ha; and he smelleth the
    battle afar off,
The thunder of the captains, and the shouting.

Doth the hawk fly by thy wisdom,
And stretch her wings toward the south ?

Doth the eagle mount up at thy command,
And make her a nest on high ?

She dwelleth and abideth on the rock,
Upon the crag of the rock, and the strong place.

From thence she seeketh the prey,
And her eyes behold afar off.

.   .   .   .   .

Then Job answered the Lord, and said,

Behold, I am vile; what shall I answer thee ?
I will lay mine hand upon my mouth.

Once have I spoken; but I will not answer:
Yea, twice; but I will proceed no further.

                              From the Book of Job.

YELLOW EYES

BLENDED by fading moonlight with the grass—
　The long brown grass that bends beneath the dew—
Supple, subtle, and silent: eyes of brass
　That rove in solemn fierceness o'er the view;
Seeking his living by the shadowed walks
Of sleeping man, Ingwi the Leopard stalks.

Thing from the utter silence of the wild,
　Thing from the outer darkness of the night,
Father of terror, of grey fear the child,
　Ingwi (in peace softer than silk; in fight
Harder than steel) cringing in fear, draws nigh
To stay his hunger where the White Men lie.

The chickens huddle in an abject dread—
　A dread no more than he, the Hunter, knows,
Yet quenches, and goes in to seek his bread
　Within the precincts of the wired close.
Goes in . . . and sudden finds that he has bought
His life to lose his life—that he is caught.

The weighted door has closed, and he is trapped . . .
　Gods of the Wilderness, what agony!
Dumbly he noses where the wires mapped
　Against the darkness show where all is free.
Dumbly he strives to stretch a fore-paw through
To touch the long grass, bending with the dew.

Dumbly he yearns toward the outer black,
　(His moon, that has sunk down for ever now,)
He sees a rabbit loping down the track,
　And hears the chilly night-breeze lisp and sough,

Lisp in the leaves that were his but this day
And now seem leagues, and countless leagues, away.

Far, far away the brooding mountains lie,
    The silver streams that croon among the ferns,
The wide umsasas black against the sky,
    The dreaming valleys where the glow-worm burns.
The veld has vanished with the closing door,
The veld that shall be Ingwi's never more.

The flash of lights—the shouts of men awake!
    And like a thunderbolt he strikes the wire,
Struggling in fury for his life's own sake;
    Wrapped in a whirling madness of desire,
Gathering his mighty power in his rage,
With thrice-fold strength he tears away the cage.

He fights, and he is free; the door is down;
    The great dogs are upon him in a breath—
Great hunters—but the half-bred boar-hound brown
    Falls struggling in the sobbing throes of death;
And Flo, his mate, her neck ripped half away,
Sinks dead before this Fury brought to bay.

Gods of the Wilderness, Ingwi is free!
    The rabbit flies in ecstasy of fear,
And Ingwi seeks that place where he would be—
    Where neither man nor animal shall peer.
Coughing the choking life-blood as he goes,
He seeks a hidden death-bed that he knows.

Blended by coming dawn-light with the ground
    That drinks his crimson power as it drips;
Seeking his chosen hiding without sound,
    Though dry with suffering are his burning lips;

Silent and savage 'neath the paling sky,
Riddled with shot, Ingwi goes back to die.
Kingsley Fairbridge.

63

THE TIGER

Tiger! Tiger! burning bright
In the forests of the night,
What immortal hand or eye
Could frame thy fearful symmetry ?

In what distant deeps or skies
Burnt the fire of thine eyes ?
On what wings dare he aspire ?
What the hand dare seize the fire ?

And what shoulder and what art
Could twist the sinews of thy heart ?
And, when thy heart began to beat,
What dread hand ? and what dread feet ?

What the hammer ?   What the chain ?
In what furnace was thy brain ?
What the anvil ?   What dread grasp
Dare its deadly terrors clasp ?

When the stars threw down their spears,
And watered heaven with their tears,
Did He smile His work to see ?
Did He who made the lamb make thee ?

Tiger! Tiger! burning bright
In the forests of the night,

What immortal hand or eye
Dare frame thy fearful symmetry ?

William Blake.

64

THE CAPTIVE LION

SUNSET—and his anxious eyes
Cannot see the golden skies,
Through the sombre iron bars
Cannot see the early stars.
In his grieving heart he sees
Lichen-waving cedar trees
On the mountains where no more
Bursts the thunder of his roar.

Evening—save cicada cries,
Silence on the forest lies.
Antelope, long-limbed and fleet,
In a watchful, swift retreat
Leave their pastures in the hills,
And the twilight coolness spills
In the lonely cedar glades,
And the paling sunlight fades.

Night-time—and his pride and he
At their hunting now would be:
Tawny shadows amber-eyed,
Heavy-shouldered, supple-thighed.
Moonrise! Time to make a kill!
Through the town, secure and still,
Sounds his deep, despairing cry,
Protest at captivity.

June Daly.

BONGWI

A HAUNTED soul put under ban,
  A hunted beast that has to roam,
The voiceless image of a man
  With neither speech nor home—

Upon the summit of the height,
  Where only wind-swept lichens grow,
Bongwi, lit by the dawning-light,
  Watches the plain below.

Fierce eyes, low brow, protruding mouth,
  Short hands that twitch and twitch again,
The hairy gargoyle of the South—
  A man without a brain!

Upon the highest krantz he waits
  Dim-lit by golden streak of dawn,
Guarding the interests of his mates
  Who wreck the fields of corn.

Far down the mealie gardens lie,
  And he, a patient sentinel,
Shouts, " Boor-hoom! " to the offended sky
  To show that all is well.

A white fish-eagle sails along,
  His mighty pinions harping tunes
Till dawn throbs with Aeolian song ;
  And, far below, the brown baboons

Look up and note the paling East,
  The fading moon, the stars that wane,
And, gorged, they quit their stolen feast
  And seek the open veld again.

And Bongwi sees.   But turns his view,
   Brown-eyed, towards the breaking morn,
And gazes through the soundless blue,
   The golden distance of the dawn.
                              Kingsley Fairbridge.

66

A FRANCISCAN PRAYER

WHEN we are past
Woodlands and moonshine nights—
Consume them not nor in the dust-wrack cast!
Save them for bat and owl,
And all night beasts that prowl,
And for night-warbling birds therein to sing
All an eternal Spring!

When we are past
Fresh uplands, flaming dawns—
Consume them not nor in the dust-wrack cast!
Save them for horse and hound,
Elm rooks and larks a-ground,
And for the proud red cocks therein to crow
An East's abiding glow!

When we are past
Bare veld and breadths of sky—
Consume them not nor in the dust-wrack cast!
Save them for all shy things
Fleet-footed, wild of wings—
To hold thanksgiving there, as well they may,
That we are gone for aye!
                              Arthur Shearly Cripps.

67

THE ALBATROSS

Now far along the skyline, like a white
Signal of triumph through the muffled light,
An Albatross, wheeling in awful rings,
Spanned the serene horizon with his wings,
And towering upwards on his scythes of fire,
Smote the thick air, that, strung with beams of light,
Clanged to his harpings like a smitten lyre
Tolling the solemn death-knell of the Night.
Till, rearing higher, he caught the blinding glow
Of sunlight frozen in his plumes of snow,
As his ethereal silver soared to fade
Into the light its own white wings had made,
And, fusing slowly, Albatross and sun
Mingled their two faint radiances in one.

From " The Flaming Terrapin,"
Roy Campbell.

68

HORSES ON THE CAMARGUE

In the grey wastes of dread,
The haunt of shattered gulls where nothing moves
But in a shroud of silence like the dead,
I heard a sudden harmony of hooves,
And, turning, saw afar
A hundred snowy horses unconfined,
The silver runaways of Neptune's car
Racing, spray-curled, like waves before the wind.
Sons of the Mistral, fleet
As him with whose strong gusts they love to flee,
Who shod the flying thunders on their feet
And plumed them with the snortings of the sea;

81

Theirs is no earthly breed
Who only haunt the verges of the earth
And only on the sea's salt herbage feed—
Surely the great white breakers gave them birth.
For when for years a slave,
A horse of the Camargue, in alien lands,
Should catch some far-off fragrance of the wave
Carried far inland from his native sands,
Many have told the tale
Of how in fury, foaming at the rein,
He hurls his rider; and with lifted tail,
With coal-red eyes and cataracting mane,
Heading his course for home,
Though sixty foreign leagues before him sweep,
Will never rest until he breathes the foam
And hears the native thunder of the deep.
But when the great gusts rise
And lash their anger on these arid coasts,
When the scared gulls career with mournful cries
And whirl across the waste like driven ghosts:
When hail and fire converge,
The only souls to which they strike no pain
Are the white-crested fillies of the surge
And the white horses of the windy plain.
Then in their strength and pride
The stallions of the wilderness rejoice;
They feel their Master's trident in their side,
And high and shrill they answer to his voice.
With white tails smoking free,
Long streaming manes, and arching necks, they show
Their kinship to their sisters of the sea—
And forward hurl their thunderbolts of snow.
Still out of hardship bred,
Spirits of power and beauty and delight
Have ever on such frugal pastures fed
And loved to course with tempests through the night.

Roy Campbell.

THREE SHIPS

WHITE Christmas, and a frosty sky
  Above the shores of Zuyder Zee;
Soft voices carol songs of peace,
  Sweet bells intone in euphony;
But there are darkened hearths to-night
  And empty homes, and friends who weep
As, ghost-like, through the starry night,
   O'er the chill bosom of the deep
    Three ships are sailing.

Like Sirens o'er the rifted seas,
  Strange fates, impenetrably veiled,
Called to these simple souls and rude
  Who sailed, nor knew to what they sailed.
Wild tales the *Haarlem's* seamen brought
  Of flowered shore, of radiant sky,
Had made a freight of dreams, and so—
    Three ships were sailing.

The women turned their treasures o'er
  And mourned old ways, as women do;
They dreamed, fear-haunted in the dark,
  Of dangers that they never knew;
But sought for guidance, as of old
  The shepherds sought the manger's light,
And so our nation's life began
   When, on our Saviour's birthday night,
    Three ships went sailing.

            Olive R. Bridgman.

SIMON VAN DER STEL

SOUTHWARD ever the Dutchmen steered,
  Southward with right good will.
No more the sea-worn sailor feared
  The Cape of Table Hill.
No longer frowned the savage land
  With famine fierce and fell,
For bounteous were the heart and hand
  Of Simon van der Stel.

Not as the rest, for greed of spoil,
  He ruled by Table Bay.
In new-built barn and seeded soil
  His little kingdom lay.
Cornfield and garden, oak and vine,
  He loved and tended well.
" Who plants a tree is friend of mine,"
  Quoth Simon van der Stel.

All in a pleasant vale was laid
  The dorp that bears his name,
With bough of fruit and leaf of shade
  To bless the founder's aim.
Here oft he sat in simple state,
  A kindly tale to tell,
And children kept the birthday fête
  Of Simon van der Stel.

Yet not beside the guarded Cape
  His narrowed fancy dwelt;
Not only in the golden grape
  Was all the flame he felt.

He knew the thought that feeds and fills,
　The ceaseless northward spell;
Three hundred miles to the Copper Hills
　Rode Simon van der Stel.

The exiles of the frugal French
　A southern refuge sought;
He bade them prove, by hedge and trench,
　The skill their fathers taught.
He watched his race of sturdy boers,
　He saw their numbers swell;
" Send wives for lusty bachelors,"
　Wrote Simon van der Stel.

Full thirty years her quiet charm
　The Cape-land o'er him cast,
Till at Constantia's favoured farm
　He turned to rest at last.
The builders from the *Haarlem* wreck
　Dug deep and founded well;
But chief of all their work to deck
　Was Simon van der Stel.

True statesman of that elder day,
　The Dutchmen's praise be thine!
Nor lesser claim need Britons lay
　To kinship of thy line.
Two races at our councils sit,
　One nation yet to dwell;
And both are heirs, by worth and wit,
　Of Simon van der Stel.

Lance Fallaw.

THE SETTLERS

How green the earth, how blue the sky,
How pleasant all the days that pass,
Here, where the British settlers lie
Beneath their cloaks of grass!

Here ancient peace resumes her round,
And rich from toil stand hill and plain;
Men reap and store: but they sleep sound,
The men who sowed the grain.

Hard to the plough their hands they put,
And wheresoe'r the soil had need
The furrows drave: and underfoot
They sowed themselves for seed.

Ah! not like him whose hand made yield
The brazen kine with fiery breath,
And over all the Colchian field
Strewed far the seeds of death—

Till, as day sank, awoke to war
The seedlings of the dragon's teeth:
And death ran multiplied once more
Across the hideous heath.

But rich in flocks be all these farms,
And fruitful be the fields which hide
Brave eyes that loved the light, and arms
That never clasped a bride!

O willing hearts turned quick to clay,
Glad lovers holding death in scorn,
Out of the lives ye cast away
The coming race is born.

Laurence Housman.

72

THOMAS PRINGLE

(Poet; and leader of the Scottish section of the 1820 Settlers.)

A fighter thou, with never time
To build the deathless rhyme:
Thine the flung gauntlet of a righteous hate;
And thine a flower of song to lone ways consecrate.

Coleridge is pleased; Sir Walter found
Romance on other ground
Than that dyed red by Gael and Saxon feud—
Romance of far horizons, sun, and solitude.

And some are listening yet: they see
Thy gallant company
Watching the hills of Scotland fade away
For ever!   Eyes unused to weeping weep that day.

But the loved notes of David's lyre,
And thine, their hearts inspire.
Whom ocean daunts not (though in craft so small
To toss for ninety days!) shall Africa appal?

Ever the Cape, to wave-tired eyes,
Appears a paradise:
To them (with yellow flag) forbidden land!
Buffeting on, they gain Algoa's barren strand.

Boldest of pioneers, Godspeed!
May courage equal need!
Trek to Glen Lynden; deem your perils o'er;
—Until by floods bereft of all your humble store.

. . . .

"Therefore his life was failure !" say
Those who but count the pay.
Fools!   From the world's so-coveted renown
God ever saveth some for His own Hand to crown.

But did he fail ?   Stars rise and set,
Their glory we forget;
His candle shineth with a steady flame;
A hundred stormy years extinguish not his fame;

For all men praise his hate of wrong,
And some his veld-flower song.
What matters it if now the petals fade ?
Not so thy name, true knight—unbought and unafraid.
                                        Arthur Vine Hall.

73

EMIGRANTS' SONG

"Our native Land—our native Vale—
    A long, a last adieu !
Farewell to bonny Lynden-dale,
    And Cheviot-mountains blue !
Farewell, ye hills of glorious deeds,
    And streams renowned in song;
Farewell, ye blithesome braes and meads
    Our hearts have loved so long.

"Farewell, ye broomy elfin knowes,
    Where thyme and harebells grow;
Farewell, ye hoary haunted howes,
    O'erhung with birk and sloe.

The battle-mound, the Border-tower,
  That Scotia's annals tell;
The martyr's grave, the lover's bower—
  To each—to all—farewell!

"Home of our hearts! our fathers' home!
  Land of the brave and free!
The keel is flashing through the foam
  That bears us far from thee:
We seek a wild and distant shore
  Beyond the Atlantic main;
We leave thee to return no more,
  Nor view thy cliffs again;

"But may dishonour blight our fame,
  And quench our household fires,
When we, or ours, forget thy name,
  Green Island of our Sires!
Our native Land—our native Vale—
  A long, a last adieu!
Farewell to bonny Lynden-dale,
  And Scotland's mountains blue."

Thomas Pringle.

74

THE FAR-FARERS

THE broad sun,
  The bright day:
White sails
  On the blue bay:
The far-farers
  Draw away.

Light the fires
    And close the door.
To the old homes,
    To the loved shore,
The far-farers
    Return no more.

                    R. L. Stevenson.

75

PIONEER'S EPITAPH

THE mills, with measured, rhythmic beat,
May, ceaseless, stamp their thousand feet
    Year after year;
" Deeps " may give place to " deeper deeps "—
Here, heedless by his outcrop, sleeps
    A pioneer.

                    William Blane.

76

DAVID LIVINGSTONE

(Buried in Westminster Abbey, April 18, 1874)

Droop, half-mast colours ; bow, bare-headed crowds,
    As this plain coffin o'er the side is slung,
To pass by woods of masts and ratlined shrouds,
    As erst by Afric's trunks liana-hung.

'Tis the last mile, of many thousands trod
    With failing strength but never-failing will,
By the worn frame, now at its rest with God,
    That never rested from its fight with ill.

·   ·   ·   ·   ·

Open the Abbey doors, and bear him in
  To sleep with king and statesman, chief and sage,
The Missionary, come of weaver-kin,
  But great by work that brooks no lower wage.

He needs no epitaph to guard a name
  Which men shall prize while worthy work is known;
He lived and died for good—be that his fame:
  Let marble crumble: this is LIVING-STONE.

                    From *Punch* (April 25, 1874).

77

VOORTREKKERS

OVER the silent horizons,
In the unknown,
There was a country that called them,
Lovely and lone.

Distant, unknown, lay the country,
Danger between;
They took their wagons and oxen
And sought the unseen.

Farther they travelled and farther;
Paused from their quest.
Still came a voice from the distance:
" Not there is rest."

They are dead and all countries discovered.
Now but in thought
Beckons that fugitive beauty,
Still to be sought.

A country of peace and attainment
Smiles to the sun,
Beckoning, beckoning,
Not to be won.

Charles Ould.

78

THE VOORTREKKER

THERE in an ancient, weather-beaten chair
He sits and ponders, drawing at the stem
Of his long-cherished pipe, his shrunken limbs
Clad loosely in a suit of yellow-grey.
His flowing beard, like flakes of falling snow,
Softens the contour of his shrewd old face,
Seamed with the touch of sun, and wind, and time,
And yet impassive.   But his shrunken eyes,
Roving and restless, seem to leap beyond,
Pregnant with all that filled forgotten years;
And for a moment he is young again.
Gripping his stick, he sits erect, the while
He doffs the clinging mask of honoured age,
As scene succeeds to scene—now gay, now grave—
The laager where he stood a puny child,
And standing, trembling, watched his father die;
And late, too late, the Zulu legions hurled,
Reeling and broken—or the gladsome days
Of headlong, breathless rides across the veld;
The ardour of the hunter and the chase;
The spell of mighty spaces, clean, pure air,
And all the subtle, nameless joy of life,
The joy of youth when pulse to pulse beats high,
The crowning joy of love that conquers all.
And then—the semblance of his first loved vrouw
(Still dearest of the three) that softly calls :

"Man is toch laat.   Kom, myn Jacobus, kom."
At sunset even so she used to cry
Whene'er he lingered, loath to leave his toil.

·   ·   ·   ·

Slowly he knocks the ashes from the bowl,
And knocking notes—perforce—his shrivelled hand.

Denys Lefebvre.

79

TREKKERS

Trekkers! slow, slow,
In the bright day-dawn's glow.
Against the crystalled sky
Looms the white tent on high—
Patiently plodding span,
Patiently plodding man,
All that his life holds dear
Slow borne behind him there.

Slow, slow, in the clear opal glow;
What is the dawn to them ?
What the new day's birth-gem ?
What the moon's diadem ?
Naught but the day begun,
Naught but the day just done!
Trekkers! slow, slow,
Through the quick brightening glow.
Patiently plodding span,
Patiently plodding man,
Slow, slow—on to the noon they go.

Trekkers! slow, slow,
In the red sunset glow.
Dust-browned and travel-spent,
Life framed within that tent,

What is the world to them ?
What are its aims and cares ?
What are its hopes and fears ?
What the great thoughts of men ?
—Life holds nor joy nor good
Beyond the wagon-hood.

Trekkers! slow, slow,
Through the red sunset glow.
Patiently plodding span,
Patiently plodding man,
Slow, slow, out of the fading glow
Into the night they go.

Beatrice Marian Bromley.

80

TREK-LULLABY

" THE sun has set, and in the skies
The little stars now open eyes ;
'Tis time for those of babes to close,
So, sleep, sleep; while high stars keep
Watch over you, my baby.

" All day the wagons jolted on,
Thro' dust and dazzle of the sun;
But now at last, day's trek is past;
Still are wheels, no longer reels
The tent; so sleep, my baby.

" Hark ! ' Who-whoo,' say the silly owls;
' Yah-ah, yah-ah,' the jackal howls;
Breezes hustle as they rustle
Trees, where cheep birds ere they sleep;
So, sleep, my bird, my baby.

" Now darkness gathers in the trees,
Just like a swarming bunch of bees;
And brown bats shear eve's dusky hair;
The moon creeps from her nest and peeps
At you ; so sleep, my baby."

Francis Carey Slater.

81

A BALLAD OF WEENEN

" OH! where away, young rider,
  Across the trackless plain,
Who twist with frantic fingers
  A flying pony's mane,

And saddle-less would dare the way
  While yet the dawn is red ? "
" Behind, they fight a losing fight,
  Nor stay to count the dead ;

My ears are filled with horrid cries,
  My heart is sick with fears! "
" Art coward then, who leave thy friends
  To Dingaan's thirsty spears ? "

" Among the dead are those too dear
  For word of mine to tell,
Yet there they lie—and here am I
  And natheless I do well.

Through endless grassy billows,
  Where late our comrades trod,
I go to seek the living
  And leave the dead to God."

"God speed thee, gallant rider,
  For now the sun is high,
And yonder tilted wagons
  Show white against the sky;

Thy shirt is torn and bloody,
  Thy boyish face is grim,
And slowly creeps the train across
  The wide horizon's rim."

"God! Could they see the broken dead
  Before them, could they know
That I alone, perchance, am left
  To warn them of the foe!"

Oh, ruthless urged the rider
  His spent and sobbing steed.
No spur had he but sorrow,
  No lash but bitter need;

But, worn and white, and gasping,
  The reeking sides he gripped;
Two arms up-reached to help him;
  Slowly to earth he slipped.

Swift to a sheltering laager
  The tented wagons grew;
Stern, to the locked wheels' shadow
  The cunning marksmen drew.

"Now thanks to thee, young rider,
  That safe the warning sped!"
"Give God the thanks, good burghers:
  I go to meet my dead."

Olive R. Bridgman.

THREE EPISODES FROM "THE TREK"

i. THE DROUGHT BREAKS

ONWARD the trekkers toil across the plain;
Tortured by heat and thirst, they pray for rain.
Onward they struggle without hope or haste,
Whilst weird dust-devils dance across the waste,
Teasing the travellers with dry-lipped laugh,
Mirthless and menacing as ghosts at play;
And quivering heat-waves swirl like flickering chaff
Turning the dull brown plain to glimmering grey.
Siren mirages mock them on their way—
Far-flashing lakes as crystalline as dew,
Girdled with trees greener than ever grew
To lime heaven's blue-birds with their leafy charm,
And buckler-off the sun with sturdy arm.
These beckoning glories fade, and leave despair:
The sky seems blanker and the waste more bare.
At last the reckless rider of the storm
Darkens the midnight with his monstrous form.
His vivid lariat in the sky is whirled,
Round berg and kop its snaky coils are curled—
Bull-peaks and heifer-koppies are his herd.
Across the plain of heaven his steed is spurred,
Whose angry neighing wakes the sleeping world,
And, as he passes, tautened thongs of rain
Tether to heaven the avid, drinking plain.

The sleeping trekkers, tired and travel-spent,
Roused by the storm now crowd within each tent.
They revel in the thunder's crash and roar,
That jars the hills just as a rock-ribbed shore
Is jolted by a punching sea; even more
Delight they in the drumming dance of rain,

Rustling like legioned locusts o'er the plain.
Cheered by the rain-song, trekkers sleep again;
Whilst in the darkness, with unerring feet,
The raindrops hornpipe on the veld and beat
A glad tattoo upon each trekker's tent,
And seem to chant and chuckle, " Sleep content,
For here's the rain at last—the life-gift, heaven-sent."

83

ii. THE BATTLE OF VEGKOP

WITH fifty wagons a ring-fort was built,
Fifty huge wagons almost tilt to tilt,
Lashed end to end with trek-chains, and between
Wheel-spokes and in all openings thorn-trees green
Were tightly piled or woven—breastworks these
That with their long sharp stinging thorns would tease
The approaching foe.   In this embattled ring
Four wagons were drawn up to form a square;
This, with rough planks and hides for covering,
Sheltered the women, children, household gear.
Within the fort the trekkers' horses were
Carefully tethered; whilst on plain and hill
The flocks and herds were left to roam at will.

Meanwhile the trekkers and their women toiled:
Bullets were moulded; guns were cleaned and oiled;
Small buckskin bags were made for the slugs of lead,
Which, at close range, cause havoc as they spread.
Then to each man, behind the wagon-wall,
Posts were assigned where gunpowder and ball
Were placed in dishes ready to each hand.
And so that brave, resourceful little band,
When nineteenth of October showed its light,
Was ranged and ready for a ruthless fight.

The trekker camp at break of day
Was ready for the coming fray,
And presently espied
A dark advancing tide
Sweeping across the shining veld.
Then solemnly the trekkers knelt,
Their heads all bowed and bare,
While Celliers offered prayer.
Thereafter in the wagon-fence
They made a gap, and issuing thence,
Riding nor fast nor slow,
They moved to meet the foe.

As they approached the swarthy mass,
Now grimly squatting on the grass,
Potgieter made essay
The holocaust to stay,
And parleyed.   But, with cobra-hiss,
The foe leapt up, advanced; at this
To earth the trekkers sprang,
Their steady snaphaans rang!
Two raking volleys straight they poured
Into the swart and savage horde,
Then, mounting, back they rode—
While galloping to load
Their smoking muskets—and again
They turned and showered blighting rain
Upon the startled foe,
Whose coming now was slow.

Twelve volleys from the belching roer,
The trekker's trusted friend and broer,
Had rattled harshly, when
Potgieter and his men
Regained the camp—without mishap;
Right speedily they closed the gap,

Whilst loud the women sang,
Their cheering voices rang
Sweet in the mellow morning air.
Then Sarel Celliers raised a prayer,
A brave and solemn plea
To God for victory.

The trekkers then with careful toil
Their muskets cleaned from smut and oil;
While steadfast Potgieter
Around the camp did stir:
To all he uttered simple words—
For little sounds can sharpen swords—
To stimulate and cheer,
Brave words to banish fear.
Meanwhile the foe like locusts swarmed,
And steadily their legions formed
Into that half-moon shape
That stays a foe's escape:
That battle-plan of Chaka dread,
The savage bull's stupendous head,
With curving horns that close
Like pincers on their foes.
But having formed their ranks, the mass
Squatted once more upon the grass,
Safe, out of gunshot range,
To watch the foemen strange,
Whose smoking-clubs had havoc made
From further distance than the blade
Of well-hurled spear might go
And lay a foeman low.

The trekkers, now impatient, wait
Their tardy foe, for soon or late,
With shout and crash and din,
The battle must begin.

Suspense may shatter ev'n the strong,
So " Blouberg " to a whip-stick long
Fastened a kerchief red
And waved it overhead.
This invitation to a fight
Found prompt acceptance—front, left, right,
With clangour, shout and hum
The Dark battalions come.

Kilted with leopards' tails were they
And plumed with feathers long and gay,
With bushy ox-tails tied
To wrist and elbow, ankle, knee,
They came in war-like panoply,
With shields of tough ox-hide—
Long oval shields, spiked at each end—
Bucklers that needful cover lend
To warriors in fight;
Shields white-and-red each veteran bore,
While youthful wights untried in war
Had shields of black and white.
Two throwing-assegais had each
To check the foeman out of reach,
And one short stabbing spear—
Broad-bladed was this weapon dread—
A knob-kerrie with heavy head
Completes each fighter's gear.

Onward they came in war-array,
Their crest-feathers like pennons gay
A-flutter in the breeze;
Each shield was beaten like a drum,
As on they came, with hiss and hum
Like drone of distant seas.
Onward they came, now nigh and nigher,
But Potgieter still held his fire,

Till thirty paces they
Were from the trekker-camp and then
He gives his eager anxious men
The word for which they pray.

The trekkers' muskets flashed and roared
And deadly volleys were out-poured
Upon the yelling foe.
The trekker women, good at need
To help their men with word and deed,
Now hurried to and fro
To bind up wounds and guns to load;
Help from their ready fingers flowed,
From white lips words of cheer.
The muskets belched out loud and fast
Upon the foe a withering blast,
But still those foes drew near.
Vainly against each wagon-tent
The hurtling assegai was sent,
Knob-sticks were hurled in vain.
The desperate foe now bravely strove
Some shackled wagon to remove,
They strove with utmost strain;
The wagon-ring they could not break,
The sheltered Boers they failed to shake,
So vanquished, they retire;
While into them and after them
The trekkers without stay or stem
Still poured their deadly fire.

Swiftly the swarthy legions fled,
Leaving great heaps of warriors dead
Upon the blood-soaked plain.
Triumphant trekkers raised on high
Their glad hosannas to the sky
Again and yet again.

And when they saw the black cloud melt
Into the vastness of the veld,
They all, with one accord,
Knelt down and prayers of thanks did raise
And joyful hymns and psalms of praise
To Heaven's eternal Lord.

84

iii. DINGAAN'S KRAAL

UMGUNGUNDHLOVU, a huge oval kraal,
Lay on a gentle slope; a lofty wall
Of planted poles with bushes interwove
Surrounded it; before it lay a grove
Of dark-boughed trees, through which a brooklet drove
The shining share that as it furrows sings.
Within the kraal in close concentric rings
A thousand beehive huts or more found place;
Whilst in the middle of the oval space
Was a great sanctuary, a ring-fenced shrine
That held the Zulu gods—silk-coated long-horned kine.

At the high end of that huge oval stood
King Dingaan's palace.   Pillars of polished wood
Adorned with coloured beads in quaint designs
Propped up its roof of finely plaited grass.
Its earthern floor—where blood with fat combines
To form a polish—was like shining glass.
The huts of Dingaan's wives and concubines
Ringed and re-ringed his mighty palace round,
Even as high-soaring Saturn is ring-bound
By swarms of merry meteors.   Outside
The palisade rose the accursèd " Hill

Of Execution." Here the earth was dyed,
Brindled and barred by many a frozen rill
Of dried and drying blood; here human bones
Lay bleaching in the sun like useless stones,
And vultures—" Dingaan's children "—day by day
Swooped darkly down to seek their carrion-prey.

Francis Carey Slater.

85

GREEN WATERS

GREEN waters dreaming by the hill,
Green peace is mirrored in their eyes.
The quaking leaves are almost still,
So languidly the faint air sighs,
And silence like a garment lies
Upon the heart, and wraps it deep
In all the blessedness of sleep.

Once were there tumult, toil, and strife,
And men that hurried to and fro—
Blown dust along the road of life-
And brittle joy and foolish woe,
And love; but that was long ago
And here the troubled murmurs cease
Passion was there, but here is peace.

Here dwells the calm of dappled shade,
Where sunbeams slant like planted spears.
And drowsing memory has laid
Aside the burden of dead years,
And all the weight of smiles and tears,

And passion's frail and fitful gleam
Are but a dream, are but a dream.

Charles Ould.

86

ZIMBABWE

INTO the darkness whence they came
   They passed ; their country knoweth none.
They and their gods without a name
   Partake the same oblivion.
Their work they did, their work is done,
   Whose gold, it may be, shone like fire
About the brows of Solomon,
   And in the House of God's Desire.

Hence came the altar all of gold,
   The hinges of the Holy Place,
The censer with the fragrance rolled
   Skyward to seek Jehovah's face;
The golden Ark that did encase
   The Law within Jerusalem,
The lilies and the rings to grace
   The High Priest's robe and diadem.

The pestilence, the desert spear,
   Smote them; they passed, with none to tell
The names of them who laboured here:
   Stark walls and crumbled crucible,
Strait gates, and graves, and ruined well
   Abide, dumb monuments of old;
We know but that men fought and fell,
   Like us, like us, for love of Gold.

Andrew Lang.

A RHYME OF CHAMINUKA

(A wonder-worker of Mashonaland doomed to death by
Lobengula.   He is said to have foretold the coming of the
Pioneers—maybe about 7 or 8 years before they entered
Rhodesia.)

Of all whose call the Rains obeyed
Was Chaminuka best—
The Python's friend—who now has lain
Nigh threescore years at rest.

We may not doubt, we do not doubt
That Wisdom loved him well;
Those griefs we suffer day by day
Are griefs he did foretell.

He pegged a hide to stubborn rock
With pegs of yielding wood;
Mine own eyes saw that wonder wrought—
When they were young and good.

He led, we followed him, to West
At summons of a King:
He went in glee—and not in grief—
Thrumming upon a string.

'Twas when we'd met a javelined band
Beside Shangani's flood—
He muttered " On their lips is peace,
But in their eyes is Blood."

And so it was.   At break of day
They would our seer have slain:
They shot with guns: they stabbed with spears;
Yet all their toil was vain.

Deep in the earth our prophet sank:
High did he rise anew;
And—when he rose—he prophesied,
And all his words were true.

"Hither will strangers come in hosts:
Year in, year out, they'll stay:
They'll tread the people as the grass:
They'll snatch their lands away."

He sighed, "I'm weary of my life:
I dread these griefs to see:
Yet there's no man in all God's world
Fated to murder me.

No man!   Ah me!   A child maybe——"
He called a man-child near:
He gave to him a spear, and showed
Him where to drive the spear.

That spear went home: that seer went free—
Before his time—to rest
Not in our land he loved so well,
But Murder's den—to West.

He is not dust: he does but sleep
A term of years untold:

He'll wake, he'll rise—his Python's coils
Wrapt round him fold on fold—
And bring us back our rain-blest lands,
And happy homes of old.

Arthur Shearly Cripps.

88

OOM PAUL

CAST in a rugged shape, an iron mould,
Untaught, unlettered, and yet strangely wise
In reading men—their lust for power or gold
Standing revealed before those shrewd old eyes—
Knowing the weakness of a stubborn race,
And with the curb of a long-practised hand
Guiding his burghers—and in fitting place
Using the pregnant phrase they understand:
Strong with the strength of an unflinching will,
Stern as a man whose gifts with one accord
Are concentrated on one end.   Yet still,
Whether with practised tongue or naked sword,
Whether his purpose served to save or kill,
Trusting through good and evil in his Lord.

Denys Lefebvre

89

AN INSCRIPTION

TOGETHER, sundered once by blood and speech,
Joined here in equal muster of the brave,
Lie Boer and Briton, foes each worthy each:
May peace strike root into their common grave,
And, blossoming where the fathers fought and died,
Bear fruit for sons that labour side by side.

Fydell Edmund Garrett.

THE BURIAL

(C. J. RHODES, buried in the Matoppos,
April 10, 1902)

WHEN that great Kings return to clay,
 Or Emperors in their pride,
Grief of a day shall fill a day,
 Because its creature died.
But we—we reckon not with those
 Whom the mere Fates ordain,
This Power that wrought on us and goes
 Back to the Power again.

Dreamer devout, by vision led
 Beyond our guess or reach,
The travail of his spirit bred
 Cities in place of speech.
So huge the all-mastering thought that drove—
 So brief the term allowed—
Nations, not words, he linked to prove
 His faith before the crowd.

It is his will that he look forth
 Across the world he won—
The granite of the ancient North—
 Great spaces washed with sun.
There shall he patient make his seat
 (As when the Death he dared),
And there await a people's feet
 In the paths that he prepared.

There, till the vision he foresaw
 Splendid and whole arise,
And unimagined Empires draw
 To council 'neath his skies,

The immense and brooding Spirit still
    Shall quicken and control.
Living he was the land—and dead,
    His soul shall be her soul!

Rudyard Kipling.

91

THE SHANGANI MEMORIAL

WAS ever nobler grave for man than this?
Here in the quiet hills, alone, apart,
No alien sound breaking upon their rest,
No passing traffic of the feet of men—
They sleep. Their glory lives apart from them,
Throned in the hearts of grateful men; their bones,
Amid the silence of these mystic rocks,
Lie quietly here. The solitary hawk
Circles about their tomb. The soft night wind
Comes whispering up and passes; and at times
God's fury, in his thunderstorms, beats down
With pitiless might upon their resting-place,
Nor wakes them from their slumber.

                                        Oh! weep not
That in the pleasant spring-tide of their lives,
The promise of their youth unharvested,
They passed into the shadows and were gone.
Not theirs the sleepless anguish of old age,
Not theirs the bitterness of vanished hopes
And unaccomplished ends, or that long wait
For Death's mysterious call. There in hot blood,
The wine of battle coursing through their veins,
A royal anthem warm upon their lips,
Gladly they fared to Death, nor fared in vain.

That one full moment of self-sacrifice
Outweighed a thousand lives of punier men,
This noble sepulchre is worthier far
Than loftiest cathedral's marbled floor.

William Archer Way.

92

ON YOUTH STRUCK DOWN

(From an unfinished elegy)

OH ! Death, what have you to say ?
  " Like a bride—like a bridegroom they ride away :
You shall go back to make up the fire,
To learn patience—to learn grief,
To learn sleep when the light has quite gone out of your
    earthly skies,
But they have the light in their eyes
  To the end of their day."

Charlotte Mew.

93

EPILOGUE

THE rolling wheels are still; the trek is done.
No more the trekkers in the dawn-light blue
Ride through the great grey plains of the Karroo,
Where each drab koppie, dazed by the rising sun,
For a few tingling moments throbs and glows
With the red lightnings of a bursting rose:
No more in days of drought will they turn grave eyes
And prayerful lips toward the brazen skies;

The strong sun shall not smite them with his blaze,
Nor the elvish moon enchant with foam-shot rays;
Swift storms shall bellow and crash by, unheard;
Nor will the dew-song of some hidden bird
Wake them to wonder at a world new-born.
No more will they inspan in the flush of morn
To toil across the never-ending veld,
Or over some vast, rock-spiked mountain-belt
To haul their magic wagons.   Nevermore
At daybreak will they trace the fading spoor
Of buck or beast; nor will the lion's roar
Or leopard's snarl shatter their midnight sleep.
No more on galloping horses will they sweep
Over harsh plains chasing the buffalo,
Blesbok and eland, nor will their bullets bring low
The wing-foot springbok's leaping loveliness.
No more the clang of battle and the stress
Of hurtling assegai and hovering death
Stirs their brave hearts or quickens their still breath
No more when dusk comes with the whirring bat
They'll gather for the camp fire's song and chat;
And when sad night binds up day's burning scars
They'll dream no more beneath a tent of stars.

From " The Trek,"
Francis Carey Slater.

94

MY NEIGHBOUR'S LANDMARK [1]

WE bore the bound-stones from the hill
Where stone was set on stone:
We bore them—whitherward we would—
Heavily—one by one:

[1] A border beacon of an Africans' Reserve.

None other saw the deed we did
But Heaven and Earth alone.

Hidden in head-high grass she lay
That hour of noon so hot—
The brooding Earth—who never yet
Hath wrong of hers forgot:
I said, " She neither hears nor sees,
Or she regards it not."

Suddenly, where we stepped, I spied
A fresh unfathomed grave,
Whence dim and dreadful gods arose—
As once in Endor's cave—
Avenging gods—to each a stone
His brooding Mother gave.

'Twas then I saw the face of Earth—
Wrinkled and brown and dry:
She said, " An altar, God's and mine,
Were those tall stones on high:
Now shall they hang about your necks,
And drag you down to die.

In that ye bore my beacon-stones
Or many steps or few,
And made the mute cold lips to lie
That once spake only true—
For every step and every stone
Your dust to dust is due."

Arthur Shearly Cripps.

THE PACE OF THE OX

WHAT do we know (and what do we care) of Time and his
    silver scythe ?
Since there is always time to spare so long as a man's alive;
The world may come, and the world may go, and the world
    may whistle by,
But the Pace of the Ox is steady and slow, and life is a
    lullaby.

What do we know of the city's scorn, the hum of the world's
    amaze,
Hot foot haste, and the fevered dawn, and forgotten yester-
    days ?
Men may strain and women may strive in busier lands
    to-day,
But the Pace of the Ox is the pace to thrive in the land of
    veld and vlei.

Crimson dawn in the Eastern sky, purple glow in the
    West,
Thus it is that the days go by, bringing their meed of rest—
The future's hidden behind the veil, and the past—is still
    the past—
But the Pace of the Ox is the sliding scale that measures our
    work at last.

The song of the ships is far to hear, the hum of the world is
    dead,
And the lotus-life in a drowsy year is our benison instead;
Why should we push the world along, or live in a world of
    flame,
When the Pace of the Ox is steady and strong and the end
    is just the same ?

Cullen Gouldsbury.

THE SONG OF THE BUILDERS

O PEOPLE, good people,
  What news is to tell ?
Ring-a-ding-dong!   Ring-a-ding-dong!
  The building goes well.

All girt with gold from crown to hem,
  I saw great Michael stand;
The city of Jerusalem
  He bore in his right hand.

Behold these walls of stately girth,
  These towers which fall not down.
Now find for me some place on earth,
  Where I may set my town.

Upon bare earth I laid my stone;
  He set his Tower thereon,
And from its top, with trumpets blown,
  Back into heaven hath gone.

O people, good people,
  What news is to tell ?
Ring-a-ding-dong!   Ring-a-ding-dong!
  The building goes well.

                              Laurence Housman.

97

THE ROSE TREE

" O words are lightly spoken,"
Said Pearse to Connolly,
" Maybe a breath of politic words
Has withered our Rose Tree;
Or maybe but a wind that blows
Across the bitter sea."

" It needs to be but watered,"
James Connolly replied,
" To make the green come out again
And spread on every side,
And shake the blossom from the bud
To be the garden's pride."

" But where can we draw water,"
Said Pearse to Connolly,
" When all the wells are parched away?
O plain as plain can be
There's nothing but our own red blood
Can make a right Rose Tree."

W. B. Yeats.

98

TO THE SPRINGBOKS IN ENGLAND, 1932

Remember all our sacred things!
But first the Sun, our absent Sire,
Who built you bodies out of fire,
And tempered them in frosty springs;
Be like our native plough that drives
Its red ravines, like lanes of blood,
Through heaving waves of turf and mud;
And in this game, as in your lives,

The far horizon be your tryline—
A Globe of Fire upon the skyline
Shall be the only ball you see then,
That rolled amongst their limping pack.
Like Bruce's heart amongst the Heathen,
Hurls on your hurricane attack.

Roy Campbell.

99

SUSSEX

GOD gave all men all earth to love,
   But since our hearts are small,
Ordained for each one spot should prove
   Belovèd over all;
That as He watched Creation's birth
   So we, in godlike mood,
May of our love create our earth
   And see that it is good.

So one shall Baltic pines content,
   As one some Surrey glade,
Or one the palm-grove's droned lament
   Before Levuka's trade.
Each to his choice, and I rejoice
   The lot has fallen to me
In a fair ground—in a fair ground—
   Yea, Sussex by the sea!

No tender-hearted garden crowns,
   No bosomed woods adorn
Our blunt, bow-headed, whale-backed Downs,
   But gnarled and writhen thorn—
Bare slopes where chasing shadows skim,
   And through the gaps revealed
Belt upon belt, the wooded, dim
   Blue goodness of the Weald.

Clean of officious fence or hedge,
  Half-wild and wholly tame,
The wise turf cloaks the white cliff edge
  As when the Romans came.
What sign of those that fought and died
  At shift of sword and sword?
The barrow and the camp abide,
  The sunlight and the sward.

Here leaps ashore the full Sou'west
  All heavy-winged with brine,
Here lies above the folded crest
  The Channel's leaden line;
And here the sea-fogs lap and cling,
  And here, each warning each,
The sheep-bells and the ship-bells ring
  Along the hidden beach.

We have no waters to delight
  Our broad and brookless vales—
Only the dewpond on the height
  Unfed, that never fails,
Whereby no battered herbage tells
  Which way the season flies—
Only our close-bit thyme that smells
  Like dawn in Paradise.

Here through the strong unhampered days
  The tinkling silence thrills;
Or little, lost, Down churches praise
  The Lord who made the hills:
But here the Old Gods guard their round,
  And, in her secret heart,
The heathen kingdom Wilfrid found
  Dreams, as she dwells, apart.

Though all the rest were all my share,
  With equal soul I'd see
Her nine-and-thirty sisters fair,
  Yet none more fair than she.
Choose ye your need from Thames to Tweed,
  And I will choose instead
Such lands as lie 'twixt Rake and Rye,
  Black Down and Beachy Head.

I will go out against the sun
  Where the rolled scarp retires,
And the Long Man of Wilmington
  Looks naked toward the shires;
And east till doubling Rother crawls
  To find the fickle tide,
By dry and sea-forgotten walls,
  Our ports of stranded pride.

I will go north about the shaws
  And the deep ghylls that breed
Huge oaks and old, the which we hold
  No more than " Sussex weed ";
Or south where windy Piddinghoe's
  Begilded dolphin veers,
And black beside wide-bankèd Ouse
  Lie down our Sussex steers.

So to the land our hearts we give
  Till the sure magic strike,
And Memory, Use, and Love make live
  Us and our fields alike—
That deeper than our speech and thought,
  Beyond our reason's sway,
Clay of the pit whence we were wrought
  Yearns to its fellow-clay.

God gives all men all earth to love,
    But since man's heart is small
Ordains for each one spot shall prove
    Belovèd over all.
Each to his choice, and I rejoice
    The lot has fallen to me
In a fair ground—in a fair ground—
    Yea, Sussex by the sea!

Rudyard Kipling.

100

I TRAVELLED AMONG UNKNOWN MEN

I TRAVELLED among unknown men,
    In lands beyond the sea;
Nor, England! did I know till then
    What love I bore to thee.

'Tis past, that melancholy dream!
    Nor will I quit thy shore
A second time; for still I seem
    To love thee more and more.

Among thy mountains did I feel
    The joy of my desire;
And she I cherished turned her wheel
    Beside an English fire.

Thy mornings showed, thy nights concealed
    The bowers where Lucy played;
And thine too is the last green field
    That Lucy's eyes surveyed.

William Wordsworth.

101

ENGLAND

No lovelier hills than thine have laid
  My tired thoughts to rest;
No peace of lovelier valleys made
  Like peace within my breast.

Thine are the woods whereto my soul,
  Out of the noontide beam,
Flees for a refuge green and cool
  And tranquil as a dream.

Thy breaking seas like trumpets peal;
  Thy clouds—how oft have I
Watched their bright towers of silence steal
  Into infinity!

My heart within me faints to roam
  In thought even far from thee:
Thine be the grave whereto I come,
  And thine my darkness be.

Walter de la Mare.

102

AFTER THREE YEARS

(To an Essex Village)

O FIELDS and little street and faces kind,
How are you changed and I!
You, that three years this day I left behind
Beneath a sobbing sky.

We meet no more.

Time's growth and Time's decay
Re-fashion hearts and scene:
We cannot meet again: we are to-day
Other than we have been.

Those were our sires who took their long farewell
Three years agone, but we—
For love of them that loved each other well—
Yearn yet across the sea.

Arthur Shearly Cripps.

103

EXILE IN AUGUST

OVER the hills, beyond the rivers far,
Shines in the feverish night a southward star.
Somewhere beneath it surely winter clings
About my southern home, and this month there
The trees are bright with blood-red blossomings,
But lack their leaves as yet.   O God, to go
Southward ere yet September's showers be here,
Ere yet our southern hills catch fire, and glow
With flaming lilac, rose, and bronze and green,
Ere yet grow brown our bushes' silvery sheen,
Ere yet the swallows bring our summer nigh!
O but to come next month some night of stars,
And hear the drums of peace, and know one's wars
Were o'er and done!   To see against the sky
My own thatched hut stand up, and clambering
Up granite stairs, keep vigil with the stars
All one woodfire-lit night before I die!

Arthur Shearly Cripps.

ON MALVERN HILL

A WIND is brushing down the clover,
  It sweeps the tossing branches bare,
Blowing the poising kestrel over
  The crumbling ramparts of the Caer.

It whirls the scattered leaves before us
  Along the dusty road to home,
Once it awakened into chorus
  The heart-strings in the ranks of Rome.

There by the gusty coppice border
  The shrilling trumpets broke the halt,
The Roman line, the Roman order,
  Swayed forwards to the blind assault.

Spearman and charioteer and bowman
  Charged and were scattered into spray ;
Savage and taciturn, the Roman
  Hewed upwards in the Roman way.

There—in the twilight—where the cattle
  Are lowing home across the fields,
The beaten warriors left the battle
  Dead on the clansmen's wicker shields.

The leaves whirl in the wind's riot
  Beneath the Beacon's jutting spur,
Quiet are clan and chief, and quiet
  Centurion and signifer.

                              John Masefield.

PUCK'S SONG

SEE you the ferny ride that steals
Into the oak-woods far ?
O that was whence they hewed the keels
That rolled to Tràfalgar.

And mark you where the ivy clings
To Bayham's mouldering walls ?
O there we cast the stout railings
That stand around St. Paul's.

See you the dimpled track that runs
All hollow through the wheat ?
O that was where they hauled the guns
That smote King Philip's fleet.

Out of the Weald, the secret Weald,
Men sent in ancient years
The horse-shoes red at Flodden Field,
The arrows at Poitiers.

See you our little mill that clacks,
So busy by the brook ?
She has ground her corn and paid her tax
Ever since Domesday Book.

See you our stilly woods of oak ?
And the dread ditch beside ?
O that was where the Saxons broke
On the day that Harold died.

See you the windy levels spread
About the gates of Rye ?
O that was where the Northmen fled,
When Alfred's ships came by.

See you our pastures wide and lone,
Where the red oxen browse?
O there was a City thronged and known,
Ere London boasted a house.

And see you, after rain, the trace
Of mound and ditch and wall?
O that was a Legion's camping place
When Caesar sailed from Gaul.

And see you marks that show and fade
Like shadows on the Downs?
O they are the lines the Flint Men made,
To guard their wondrous towns.

Trackway and Camp and City lost,
Salt Marsh where now is corn;
Old Wars, old Peace, old Arts that cease,
And so was England born!

She is not any common Earth,
Water or wood or air,
But Merlin's Isle of Gramarye,
Where you and I will fare.

Rudyard Kipling.

106

PORTRAIT OF A WARRIOR

His brow is seamed with line and scar;
  His cheek is red and dark as wine;
The fires as of a Northern star
  Beneath his cap of sable shine.

His right hand, bared of leathern glove,
   Hangs open like an iron gin,
You stoop to see his pulses move,
   To hear the blood sweep out and in.

He looks some king, so solitary
   In earnest thought he seems to stand,
As if across a lonely sea
   He gazed impatient of the land.

Out of the noisy centuries
   The foolish and the fearful fade;
Yet burn unquenched these warrior eyes,
   Time hath not dimmed nor death dismayed.

Walter de la Mare.

107

A BALLAD OF THE FLEET

At Flores in the Azores Sir Richard Grenville lay,
And a pinnace, like a fluttered bird, came flying from far
   away:
" Spanish ships of war at sea! we have sighted fifty-three! "
Then swore Lord Thomas Howard: " 'Fore God I am no
   coward;
But I cannot meet them here, for my ships are out of gear,
And the half my men are sick. I must fly, but follow
   quick.
We are six ships of the line; can we fight with fifty-
   three ? "

Then spake Sir Richard Grenville: "I know you are no
    coward;
You fly them for a moment to fight with them again.
But I've ninety men and more that are lying sick ashore.
I should count myself the coward if I left them, my Lord
    Howard,
To these Inquisition dogs and the devildoms of Spain."

So Lord Howard passed away with five ships of war that
    day,
Till he melted like a cloud in the silent summer heaven;
But Sir Richard bore in hand all his sick men from the
    land
Very carefully and slow,
Men of Bideford in Devon,
And we laid them on the ballast down below;
For we brought them all aboard,
And they blest him in their pain, that they were not left to
    Spain,
To the thumbscrew and the stake, for the glory of the
    Lord.

He had only a hundred seamen to work the ship and to
    fight,
And he sailed away from Flores till the Spaniard came in
    sight,
With his huge sea-castles heaving upon the weather bow.
" Shall we fight or shall we fly ?
Good Sir Richard, tell us now,
For to fight is but to die!
There'll be little of us left by the time this sun be set."
And Sir Richard said again: " We be all good English
    men.
Let us bang these dogs of Seville, the children of the devil,
For I never turned my back upon Don or devil yet."

Sir Richard spoke and he laughed, and we roared a hurrah, and so

The little *Revenge* ran on sheer into the heart of the foe,

With her hundred fighters on deck, and her ninety sick below;

For half of their fleet to the right and half to the left were seen,

And the little *Revenge* ran on through the long sea-lane between.

Thousands of their soldiers looked down from their decks and laughed,

Thousands of their seamen made mock at the mad little craft

Running on and on, till delayed

By their mountain-like *San Philip* that, of fifteen hundred tons,

And up-shadowing high above us with her yawning tiers of guns,

Took the breath from our sails, and we stayed.

And while now the great *San Philip* hung above us like a cloud

Whence the thunderbolt will fall

Long and loud,

Four galleons drew away

From the Spanish fleet that day,

And two upon the larboard and two upon the starboard lay,

And the battle-thunder broke from them all.

But anon the great *San Philip*, she bethought herself and went,

Having that within her womb that had left her ill content;

And the rest they came aboard us, and they fought us hand to hand,

For a dozen times they came with their pikes and mus-
queteers,
And a dozen times we shook 'em off as a dog that shakes his
ears
When he leaps from the water to the land.

And the sun went down, and the stars came out far over
the summer sea,
But never a moment ceased the fight of the one and the
fifty-three.
Ship after ship, the whole night long, their high-built
galleons came,
Ship after ship, the whole night long, with her battle-
thunder and flame;
Ship after ship, the whole night long, drew back with her
dead and her shame.
For some were sunk and many were shattered, and so could
fight us no more—
God of battles, was ever a battle like this in the world
before ?

For he said, " Fight on! fight on! "
Though his vessel was all but a wreck;
And it chanced that, when half of the short summer night
was gone,
With a grisly wound to be dressed he had left the deck,
But a bullet struck him that was dressing it suddenly dead,
And himself he was wounded again in the side and the
head,
And he said, " Fight on! fight on! "

And the night went down, and the sun smiled out far over
the summer sea,
And the Spanish fleet with broken sides lay round us all in a
ring;

But they dared not touch us again, for they feared that we
    still could sting,
So they watched what the end would be.
And we had not fought them in vain,
But in perilous plight were we,
Seeing forty of our poor hundred were slain,
And half of the rest of us maimed for life
In the crash of the cannonades and the desperate strife;
And the sick men down in the hold were most of them
    stark and cold,

And the pikes were all broken or bent, and the powder was
    all of it spent;
And the masts and the rigging were lying over the side;
But Sir Richard cried in his English pride:
" We have fought such a fight for a day and a night
As may never be fought again!
We have won great glory, my men!
And a day less or more
At sea or ashore,
We die—does it matter when ?
Sink me the ship, Master Gunner—sink her, split her in
    twain!
Fall into the hands of God, not into the hands of Spain!"

And the gunner said, " Ay, ay," but the seamen made
    reply:
" We have children, we have wives,
And the Lord hath spared our lives.
We will make the Spaniard promise, if we yield, to let us
    go;
We shall live to fight again and to strike another blow."
And the lion there lay dying, and they yielded to the foe.

And the stately Spanish men to their flagship bore him then
Where they laid him by the mast, old Sir Richard caught
   at last,
And they praised him to his face with their courtly foreign
   grace;
But he rose upon their decks, and he cried:
" I have fought for Queen and Faith like a valiant man and
   true;
I have only done my duty as a man is bound to do:
With a joyful spirit I, Sir Richard Grenville, die! "
And he fell upon their decks, and he died.

And they stared at the dead that had been so valiant and
   true,
And had holden the power and glory of Spain so cheap
That he dared her with one little ship and his English few;
Was he devil or man ?   He was devil for aught they knew,
But they sank his body with honour down into the deep;
And they manned the *Revenge* with a swarthier alien crew,
And away she sailed with her loss and longed for her own;
When a wind from the lands they had ruined awoke from
   sleep,
And the water began to heave and the weather to moan,
And or ever that evening ended a great gale blew,
And a wave like the wave that is raised by an earthquake
   grew,
Till it smote on their hulls and their sails and their masts
   and their flags,
And the whole sea plunged and fell on the shot-shattered
   navy of Spain,
And the little *Revenge* herself went down by the island
   crags
To be lost evermore in the main.

                        Lord Tennyson.

YE MARINERS OF ENGLAND

Yᴇ Mariners of England
  That guard our native seas!
Whose flag has braved, a thousand years,
  The battle and the breeze!
Your glorious standard launch again
  To match another foe;
And sweep through the deep,
  While the stormy winds do blow;
While the battle rages loud and long
  And the stormy winds do blow.

The spirits of your fathers
  Shall start from every wave—
For the deck it was their field of fame,
  And Ocean was their grave:
Where Blake and mighty Nelson fell
  Your manly hearts shall glow,
As ye sweep through the deep,
  While the stormy winds do blow;
While the battle rages loud and long
  And the stormy winds do blow.

Britannia needs no bulwarks,
  No towers along the steep;
Her march is o'er the mountain waves,
  Her home is on the deep.
With thunders from her native oak
  She quells the floods below,
As they roar on the shore,
  When the stormy winds do blow;
When the battle rages loud and long,
  And the stormy winds do blow.

The meteor flag of England
  Shall yet terrific burn;
Till danger's troubled night depart
  And the star of peace return.
Then, then ye ocean-warriors!
  Our song and feast shall flow
To the fame of your name,
  When the storm has ceased to blow;
When the fiery fight is heard no more,
  And the storm has ceased to blow.

Thomas Campbell.

109

THE PLOUGH

A Landscape in Berkshire

Above yon sombre swell of land
  Thou see'st the dawn's grave orange hue,
With one pale streak like yellow sand,
  And over that a vein of blue.

The air is cold above the woods;
  All silent is the earth and sky,
Except with his own lonely moods
  The blackbird holds a colloquy.

Over the broad hill creeps a beam,
  Like hope that gilds a good man's brow;
And now ascends the nostril-steam
  Of stalwart horses come to plough.

Ye rigid Ploughmen, bear in mind
  Your labour is for future hours:
Advance—spare not—nor look behind-
  Plough deep and straight with all your powers!

Richard Henry Horne.

THE PLOUGHMAN

UNDER the long fell's stony eaves
The ploughman, going up and down,
Ridge after ridge man's tide-mark leaves,
And turns the hard grey soil to brown.

Striding, he measures out the earth
In lines of life, to rain and sun;
And every year that comes to birth
Sees him still striding on and on.

The seasons change, and then return;
Yet still, in blind, unsparing ways,
However I may shrink or yearn,
The ploughman measures out my days.

His acre brought forth roots last year;
This year it bears the gleamy grain;
Next spring shall seedling grass appear;
Then roots and corn and grass again.

Five times the young corn's pallid green
I have seen spread and change and thrill;
Five times the reapers I have seen
Go creeping up the far-off hill:

And, as the unknowing ploughman climbs
Slowly and inveterately,
I wonder long how many times
The corn will spring again for me.

Gordon Bottomley.

TO A SKYLARK

Hail to thee, blithe spirit!—
    Bird thou never wert—
That from heaven or near it
    Pourest thy full heart
In profuse strains of unpremeditated art.

Higher still and higher
    From the earth thou springest,
Like a cloud of fire;
    The blue deep thou wingest,
And singing still dost soar, and soaring ever singest.

In the golden lightning
    Of the sunken sun,
O'er which clouds are brightening,
    Thou dost float and run,
Like an unbodied joy whose race is just begun.

The pale purple even
    Melts around thy flight ;
Like a star of heaven,
    In the broad daylight
Thou art unseen, but yet I hear thy shrill delight—

Keen as are the arrows
    Of that silver sphere
Whose intense lamp narrows
    In the white dawn clear,
Until we hardly see, we feel that it is there.

All the earth and air
  With thy voice is loud,
As, when night is bare,
  From one lonely cloud
The moon rains out her beams, and heaven is overflowed.

What thou art we know not;
  What is most like thee?
From rainbow clouds there flow not
  Drops so bright to see
As from thy presence showers a rain of melody:—

Like a poet hidden
  In the light of thought,
Singing hymns unbidden,
  Till the world is wrought
To sympathy with hopes and fears it heeded not:

Like a high-born maiden
  In a palace tower,
Soothing her love-laden
  Soul in secret hour
With music sweet as love, which overflows her bower:

Like a glow-worm golden
  In a dell of dew,
Scattering unbeholden
  Its aerial hue
Among the flowers and grass which screen it from the view.

Like a rose embowered
  In its own green leaves,
By warm winds deflowered,
  Till the scent it gives
Makes faint with too much sweet these heavy-wingèd
thieves.

Sound of vernal showers
    On the twinkling grass,
Rain-awakened flowers-
    All that ever was
Joyous, and clear, and fresh—thy music doth surpass

Teach us, sprite or bird,
    What sweet thoughts are thine:
I have never heard
    Praise of love or wine
That panted forth a flood of rapture so divine.

Chorus hymeneal,
    Or triumphal chaunt,
Matched with thine would be all
    But an empty vaunt—
A thing wherein we feel there is some hidden want.

What objects are the fountains
    Of thy happy strain ?
What fields, or waves, or mountains ?
    What shapes of sky or plain ?
What love of thine own kind ? what ignorance of pain?

With thy clear keen joyance
    Languor cannot be:
Shadow of annoyance
    Never came near thee:
Thou lovest, but ne'er knew love's sad satiety.

Waking or asleep,
    Thou of death must deem
Things more true and deep
    Than we mortals dream,
Or how could thy notes flow in such a crystal stream ?

We look before and after,
  And pine for what is not:
Our sincerest laughter
  With some pain is fraught;
Our sweetest songs are those that tell of saddest thought.

Yet, if we could scorn
  Hate, and pride, and fear,
If we were things born
  Not to shed a tear,
I know not how thy joy we ever should come near.

Better than all measures
  Of delightful sound,
Better than all treasures
  That in books are found,
Thy skill to poet were, thou scorner of the ground!

Teach me half the gladness
  That thy brain must know;
Such harmonious madness
  From my lips would flow,
The world should listen then, as I am listening now.

                                            P. B. Shelley.

112

THE ECSTATIC

LARK, skylark, spilling your rubbed and round
Pebbles of sound in air's still lake,
Whose widening circles fill the noon; yet none
Is known so small beside the sun:

Be strong your fervent soaring, your skyward air!
Tremble there, a nerve of song!
Float up there where voice and wing are one,
A singing star, a note of light!

Buoyed, embayed in heaven's noon-wide reaches—
For soon light's tide will turn—Oh stay!
Cease not till day streams to the west, then down
That estuary drop down to peace.

C. Day Lewis.

113

COMPOSED UPON WESTMINSTER BRIDGE,
Sept. 3, 1802.

EARTH has not anything to show more fair:
Dull would he be of soul who could pass by
A sight so touching in its majesty:
This City now doth, like a garment, wear
The beauty of the morning; silent, bare,
Ships, towers, domes, theatres, and temples lie
Open unto the fields, and to the sky;
All bright and glittering in the smokeless air.
Never did sun more beautifully steep
In his first splendour, valley, rock, or hill;
Ne'er saw I, never felt, a calm so deep!
The river glideth at his own sweet will:
Dear God! the very houses seem asleep;
And all that mighty heart is lying still!

William Wordsworth.

114

INSIDE OF KING'S COLLEGE CHAPEL, CAMBRIDGE

TAX not the royal Saint with vain expense,
With ill-matched aims the Architect who planned—
Albeit labouring for a scanty band
Of white-robed Scholars only—this immense
And glorious work of fine intelligence!
Give all thou canst; high Heaven rejects the lore
Of nicely-calculated less or more;
So deemed the man who fashioned for the sense
These lofty pillars, spread that branching roof
Self-poised and scooped into ten thousand cells,
Where light and shade repose, where music dwells
Lingering—and wandering on as loth to die;
Like thoughts whose very sweetness yieldeth proof
That they were born for immortality.

William Wordsworth.

115

WOODWORKER'S BALLAD

ALL that is moulded of iron
Has lent to destruction and blood;
But the things that are honoured of Zion
Are most of them made from wood.

Stone can be chiselled to Beauty,
And iron shines bright for Defence;
But when Mother Earth pondered her duty
She brought forth the forest, from whence

Come tables, and chairs, and crosses,
Little things that a hot fire warps,
Old ships that the blue wave tosses,
And fiddles for music, and harps;

Oak boards where the carved ferns mingle,
Monks' shrines in the wilderness,
Snug little huts in the dingle,
All things that the sad poets bless.

King Arthur had a wood table;
And Our Lord blessed wood; for, you see,
He was born in a wooden stable,
And He died on a wooden tree;

And He sailed in a wooden vessel
On the waters of Galilee,
And He worked at a wooden trestle
At His wonderful carpentry.

Oh, all that is moulded of iron
Has lent to destruction and blood;
But the things that are honoured of Zion
Are most of them made from wood.

Herbert Edward Palmer.

116

THE BRIDGE

HERE, with one leap,
The bridge that spans the cutting; on its back
The load
Of the main road,
And under it the railway-track.

Into the plains they sweep,
Into the solitary plains asleep,
The flowing lines, the parallel lines of steel—
Fringed with their narrow grass,
Into the plains they pass,
The flowing lines, like arms of mute appeal.

A cry
Prolonged across the earth—a call
To the remote horizons and the sky;
The whole east rushes down them with its light,
And the whole west receives them, with its pall
Of stars and night—
The flowing lines, the parallel lines of steel.

And with the fall
Of darkness, see! the red,
Bright anger of the signal, where it flares
Like a huge eye that stares
On some hid danger in the dark ahead.
A twang of wire—unseen
The signal drops; and now, instead
Of a red eye, a green.

Out of the silence grows
An iron thunder—grows, and roars, and sweeps,
Menacing!   The plain
Suddenly leaps,
Startled, from its repose—
Alert and listening.   Now, from the gloom
Of the soft distance, loom
Three lights and, over them, a brush
Of tawny flame and flying spark—
Three pointed lights that rush,
Monstrous, upon the cringing dark.

And nearer, nearer rolls the sound,
Louder the throb and roar of wheels,
The shout of speed, the shriek of steam;
The sloping bank,
Cut into flashing squares, gives back the clank
And grind of metal, while the ground
Shudders and the bridge reels—
As, with a scream,
The train,
A rage of smoke, a laugh of fire,
A lighted anguish of desire,
A dream
Of gold and iron, of sound and flight,
Tumultuously roars across the night.

The train roars past—and, with a cry,
Drowned in a flying howl of wind,
Half-stifled in the smoke and blind,
The plain,
Shaken, exultant, unconfined,
Rises, flows on, and follows, and sweeps by,
Shrieking, to lose itself in distance and the sky.

J. Redwood Anderson.

117

THE SIGNALLER

HE goes.   On ledge of our wild hill he stands.
As the quiet night falls deep, his eager hands
Grow busy at his lamp: time after time
They'll beat a measure out: then times again
They'll pause, while thro' the dark his eyes will strain
At yonder ridge.   As rhyme cries out to rhyme,
As bell to bell in glee of belfry chime,

As star to morning-star in choir of old
Made music of refrain,
So lamp asks lamp with quivering tongue of gold
Its questions manifold,
Nor asks in vain.

Arthur Shearly Cripps.

118

THE EXPRESS

AFTER the first powerful plain manifesto
The black statement of pistons, without more fuss
But gliding like a queen, she leaves the station.
Without bowing and with restrained unconcern
She passes the houses which humbly crowd outside,
The gasworks and at last the heavy page
Of death, printed by gravestones in the cemetery.
Beyond the town there lies the open country
Where, gathering speed, she acquires mystery,
The luminous self-possession of ships on ocean.
It is now she begins to sing—at first quite low
Then loud, and at last with a jazzy madness—
The song of her whistle screaming at curves,
Of deafening tunnels, brakes, innumerable bolts.
And always light, aerial, underneath,
Goes the elate metre of her wheels.
Steaming through metal landscape on her lines
She plunges new eras of wild happiness
Where speed throws up strange shapes, broad curves
And parallels clean like the steel of guns.
At last, further than Edinburgh or Rome,
Beyond the crest of the world, she reaches night
Where only a low streamline brightness
Of phosphorus on the tossing hills is white.

Ah, like a comet through flame, she moves entranced
Wrapt in her music no bird song, no, nor bough
Breaking with honey buds, shall ever equal.

Stephen H. Spender.

119

SING WE THE TWO LIEUTENANTS

Sing we the two lieutenants, Parer and M'Intosh,
After the War wishing to hie them home to Australia,
Planned they would take a high way, a hazardous crazy
    air-way:
Death their foregone conclusion, a flight headlong to failure,
We said.   For no silver posh
Plane was their pigeon, no dandy dancer quick-stepping
    through heaven,
But a craft of obsolete design, a condemned D.H. nine;
Sold for a song it was, patched up though to write an heroic
Line across the world as it reeled on its obstinate stoic
Course to that southern haven.

On January 8, 1920, their curveting wheels kissed
England goodbye.   Over Hounslow huddled in morning
    mist
They rose and circled like buzzards while we rubbed our
    sleepy eyes:
Like a bird scarce-fledged they flew, whose flying hours
    are few—
Still dear is the nest but deeper its desire unto the skies—
And they left us to our sleeping.
They felt earth's warning tug on their wings: vain to
    advance
Asking a thoroughfare through the angers of the air
On so flimsy a frame: but they pulled up her nose and the
    earth went sloping
Away, and they aimed for France.

Fog first, a wet blanket, a kill-joy, the primrose-of-morn-
    ing's blight,
Blotting out the dimpled sea, the ample welcome of land,
The gay glance from the bright
Cliff-face behind, snaring the sky with treachery, sneering
At hope's loss of height. But they charged it, flying blind;
They took a compass-bearing against that dealer of doubt,
As a saint when the field of vision is fogged gloriously steels
His spirit against the tainter of air, the elusive taunter:
They climbed to win a way out,
Then downward dared till the moody waves snarled at
    their wheels.

Landing at last near Conteville, who had skimmed the crest
    of oblivion,
They could not rest, but rose and flew on to Paris, and there
Trivially were delayed—a defective petrol feed—
Three days: a time hung heavy on
Hand and heart, till they leapt again to the upper air,
Their element, their lover, their angel antagonist.
Would have taken a fall without fame, but the sinewy
    framework the wrist
Of steel the panting engine wrestled well: and they went
South while the going was good, as a swallow that guide
    nor goad
Needs on his sunny scent.

At Lyons the petrol pump failed again, and forty-eight
    hours
They chafed to be off, the haughty champions whose
    breathing-space
Was an horizon span and the four winds their fan.
Over Italy's shores
A reverse, the oil ran out and cursing they turned about
Losing a hundred miles to find a landing-place.

Not a coast for a castaway this, no even chance of alighting
On sward or wind-smooth sand:
A hundred miles without pressure they flew, the engine
fighting
For breath, and its heart nearly burst before they dropped
to land.

And now the earth they had spurned rose up against them
in anger,
Tier upon tier it towered, the terrible Apennines:
No sanctuary there for wings, not flares nor landing-lines,
No hope of floor and hangar.
Yet those ice-tipped spears that disputed the passage set
spurs
To their two hundred and forty horse power; grimly they
gained
Altitude, though the hand of heaven was heavy upon them,
The downdraught from the mountains: though desperate
eddies spun them
Like a coin, yet unkindly tossed their luck came uppermost
And mastery remained.

Air was all ambushes round them, was avalanche earthquake
Quicksand, a funnel deep as doom, till climbing steep
They crawled like a fly up the face of perpendicular night
And levelled, finding a break
At fourteen thousand feet.   Here earth is shorn from sight:
Deadweight a darkness hangs on their eyelids, and they
bruise
Their eyes against a void: vindictive the cold airs close
Down like a trap of steel and numb them from head to heel;
Yet they kept an even keel,
For their spirit reached forward and took the controls while
their fingers froze.

They had not heard the last of death.   When the mountains were passed,
He raised another crest, the long crescendo of pain
Kindled to climax, the plane
Took fire.   Alone in the sky with the breath of their enemy
Hot in their face they fought: from three thousand feet they tilted
Over, side-slipped away—a trick for an ace, a race
And running duel with death: flame streamed out behind,
A crimson scarf of, as life-blood out of a wound, but the wind
Of their downfall staunched it; death wilted,
Lagged and died out in smoke—he could not stay their pace.

A lull for a while.   The powers of hell rallied their legions.
On Parer now fell the stress of the flight; for the plane had been bumped,
Buffeted, thrashed by the air almost beyond repair:
But he tinkered and coaxed, and they limped
Over the Adriatic on into warmer regions.
Erratic their course to Athens, to Crete: coolly they rode her
Like a tired horse at the water-jumps, they jockeyed her over seas,
Till they came at last to a land whose dynasties of sand
Had seen Alexander, Napoleon, many a straddling invader,
But never none like these.

England to Cairo, a joy-ride, a forty-hour journey at most,
Had cost them forty-four days.   What centuried strata of life
Fuelled the fire that haled them to heaven, the power that held them
Aloft?   For their plane was a laugh,
A patch, brittle as matchstick, a bubble, a lift for a ghost:
Bolts always working loose of propeller, cylinder, bearer;

Instruments faulty; filter, magneto, each strut unsound.
Yet after four days, though we swore she never could leave
   the ground,
We saw her in headstrong haste diminish towards the east—
That makeshift, mad sky-farer.

Aimed they now for Baghdad, unwritten in air's annals
A voyage.   But theirs the fate all flights of logic to refute,
Who obeyed no average law, who buoyed the viewless
   channels
Of sky with a courage steadfast, luminous. Safe they
   crossed
Sinai's desert, and daring
The Nejd, the unneighbourly waste of Arabia, yet higher
   soaring
(Final a fall there for birds of passage, limed and lost
In shifty the sand's embrace) all day they strove to climb
Through stormy rain: but they felt her shorten her stride
   and falter,
And they fell at evening time.

Slept that night beside their machine, and the next morning
Raider Arabs appeared reckoning this stranded bird
A gift: like cobras they struck, and their gliding shadows
   athwart
The sand were all their warning.
But the aeronauts, knowing iron the coinage here, had
   brought
Mills bombs and revolvers, and M'Intosh held them off
While Parer fought for life—
A spark, the mechanic's right answer, and finally wrought
A miracle, for the dumb engine spoke and they rose
Convulsively out of the clutch of the desert, the clench of
   their foes.

Orchestrate this theme, artificer-poet.   Imagine
The roll, crackling percussion, quickening tempo of engine
For a start: the sound as they soar, an octave-upward slur
Scale of sky ascending:
Hours-held note of level flight, a beat unhurried,
Sustaining undertone of movement never-ending:
Wind shrill on the ailerons, flutes and fifes in a flurry
Devilish when they dive, plucking of tense stays.
These hardly heard it, who were the voice, the heavenly air
That sings above always.

We have seen the extremes, the burning, the freezing, the
    outward face
Of their exploit; heroic peaks, tumbling-to-zero de-
    pressions:
Little our graph can show, the line they traced through
    space,
Of the heart's passionate patience.
How soft drifts of sleep piled on their senses deep
And they dug themselves out often: how the plane was a
    weight that hung
And swung on their aching nerve; how din drilled through
    the skull
And sight sickened—so slow earth filtered past below.
Yet nerve failed never, heart clung
To height, and the brain kept its course and the hand its skill.

Baghdad renewed a propeller damaged in desert.   Arid
Baluchistan spared them that brought down and spoilt with
    thirst
Armies of Alexander.   To Karachi they were carried
On cloud-back: fragile as tinder their plane, but the winds
    were tender
Now to their need, and nursed
Them along till teeming India made room for them to
    alight

150

Wilting her wings, the sweltering suns had moulted her
  bright
Plumage, rotten with rain
The fabric: but they packed her with iron washers and
  tacked her
Together, good for an hour, and took the air again.

Feats for a hundred flights, they were prodigal of: a fairest
Now to tell—how they foiled death when the engine failed
Above the Irrawaddy, over close-woven forest.
What shoals for a pilot there, what a snarled passage and
  dark
Shelves down to doom and grip
Of green!   But look, balanced superbly, quick off the mark
Swooping like centre three-quarter whose impetus storms
  a gap—
Defenders routed, rooted their feet, and their arms are
  mown
Aside, that high or low aim at his overthrow—
M'Intosh touched her down.

And they picked her up out of it somehow and put her at
  the air, a
Sorry hack for such steeplechasing, to leap the sky.
" We'll fly this crate till it falls to bits at our feet,"
Said the mechanic Parer.
And at Moulmein soon they crashed; and the plane by their
  spirit's high
Tension long pinned, girded and guarded from dissolution,
Fell to bits at their feet.   Wrecked was the undercarriage,
Radiator cracked, in pieces, compasses crocked;
Fallen all to confusion.
Their winged hope was a heap of scrap, but unsplintered
  their courage.

Six weeks they worked in sun-glare and jungle damps, assembling
Fragments to make airworthy what was worth not its weight in air.
As a surgeon, grafter of skin, as a setter of bones tumbling
Apart, they had power to repair
This good for naught but the grave: they livened her engine and gave
Fuselage faith to rise rejuvenated from ruin.
Went with them stowaways, not knowing what hazard they flew in—
Bear-cubs, a baby alligator, lizards and snakes galore;
Mascots maybe, for the plane though twice she was floored again
Always came up for more.

Till they came to the pitiless mountains of Timor. Yet these, untamed,
Not timorous, against the gradient and Niagara of air they climbed
Scarce-skimming the summits; and over the shark-toothed Timor sea
Lost their bearings, but shirked not the odds, the deaths that lurked
A million to one on their trail:
They reached out to the horizon and plucked their destiny.
On for eight hours they flew blindfold against the unknown,
And the oil began to fail
And their flying spirit waned—one pint of petrol remained
When the land stood up to meet them and they came into their own.

Southward still to Melbourne, the bourn of their flight, they pressed
Till at last near Culcairn, like a last fretted leaf
Falling from brave autumn into earth's breast,

D.H. nine, their friend that had seen them to the end,
Gave up her airy life.
The Southern Cross was splendid above the spot where
   she fell,
The end of her rainbow curve over our weeping day:
And the flyers, glad to be home, unharmed by that dizzy
   fall,
Dazed as the dead awoken from death, stepped out of the
   broken
Body and went away.

What happened then, the roar
   and rave of waving crowds
That fêted them, was only
   an afterglow of glory
Reflected on the clouds
   where they had climbed alone,
Day's golden epilogue:
   and them, whose meteor path
Lightened our eyes, whose great
   spirit lifted the fog
That sours a doubtful earth,
   the stars commemorate.

C. Day Lewis.

120

UNDER THE GREENWOOD TREE

UNDER the greenwood tree
Who loves to lie with me,
And turn his merry note
Unto the sweet bird's throat,
Come hither, come hither, come hither:
   Here shall he see
   No enemy
But winter and rough weather.

Who doth ambition shun,
And loves to live i' the sun,
Seeking the food he eats,
And pleased with what he gets,
Come hither, come hither, come hither:
Here shall he see
No enemy
But winter and rough weather.

William Shakespeare.

121

A BALLAD OF ROBIN HOOD

LITHE and listen, Gentlemen,
And hearken what I shall say,
How the proud Sheriff of Nottingham
Did cry a full fair play;

That all the best archers of the North
Should come upon a day,
" And he that shooteth alder-best
The game shall bear away.

" He that shooteth alder-best,
Furthest, fair, and law,
At a pair of fynly butts,
Under the green-wood shaw,

" A right good arrow he shall have,
The shaft of silver white,
The head and feathers of rich red gold,
In England is none like."

This then heardè good Robin,
Under his trystell-tree:
" Make you ready, ye wight young men;
That shooting will I see.

154

" Busk you, my merry young men,
 Ye shall go with me:
And I will wete the Sheriff's faith,
 True an if he be."

When they had their bows i-bent,
 Their tackles feathered free,
Seven score of wight young men
 Stood by Robin's knee.

When they came to Nottingham,
 The butts were fair and long;
Many was the bold archèr
 That shot with bowè strong.

" There shall but six shoot with me,
 The other shall keep my heed,
And stand with good bowès bent
 That I be not deceived."

The fourth outlaw his bow gan bend,
 And that was Robin Hood,
And that beheld the proud Sheriff,
 All by the butt he stood.

Thrice Robin shot about,
 And alway he sliced the wand,
And so did good Gilbert,
 With the white hand.

Little John and good Scathelock
 Were archers good and free;
Little Much and good Reynold,
 The worst would they not be.

When they haddè shot about,
    These archers fair and good,
Evermore was the best,
    For soothè, Robin Hood.

Him was delivered the good arròw,
    For best worthy was he;
He took the gift so courteously,
    To greenè-wood would he.

They crièd out on Robin Hood
    And great horns gan they blow:
" Woe worth thee, treason! " said Robin,
    " Full evil thou art to know.

" And woe be thee, thou proud Sheriff,
    Thus gladding thy guest;
Otherwise thou behotè me
    In yonder wild forèst.

" But had I thee in greenè-wood,
    Under my trystell-tree,
Thou shouldest leave me a better wed
    Than thy true lewtè."

Full many a bowè there was bent,
    And arrows let they glide;
Many a kirtle there was rent,
    And hurt full many a side.

The outlaws' shottè was so strong
    That no man might them drive,
And the proudè Sheriff's men
    They fled away full blive.

Robin saw the bushment broke,
    In green-wood he would be;
Many an arrow there was shot
    Among that company.

Little John was hurt full sore,
    With an arrow in his knee,
That he might neither go nor ride;
    It was full great pity.

"Master," then said Little John,
    "If ever thou lovest me,
And for that ilk Lordès love,
    That died upon a tree,

"And for the meeds of my service,
    That I have servèd thee,
Let never the proud Sheriff
    Alive now findè me;

"But take out thy brown sword,
    And smite all off my head
And give me woundes dead and wide,
    No life on me be left."

"I would not that," said Robin,
    "John, that thou were slawe,
For all the gold in merry England,
    Though it lay now in a rawe."

"God forbid," said Little Much,
    "That died on a tree,
That thou shouldest, Little John,
    Part our company."

Up Robin took him on his back,
 And bare him well a mile;
Many a time he laid him down,
 And shot another while.

Then was there a fair castèll,
 A little within the wood;
Double-ditched it was about,
 And wallèd, by the rood.

And there dwelt that gentle Knight,
 Sir Richard at the Lee,
That Robin haddè lent his good,
 Under the green-wood tree.

In he took good Robin,
 And all his company:
" Welcome be thou, Robin Hood,
 Welcome art thou to me;

" And much I thank thee of thy comfort,
 And of thy courtesy,
And of thy great kindness,
 Under the green-wood tree;

" I love no man in all this world
 So much as I do thee;
For all the proud Sheriff of Nottingham,
 Right here shalt thou be.

" Shut the gates and draw the bridge,
 And let no man come in,
And arm you well, and make you ready,
 And to the walls ye win.

"For one thing, Robin, I thee behote,
    I swear by Saint Quintin,
These twelve days thou wonest with me,
    To sup, eat, and dine."

From "A Little Geste of Robin Hood and His Meiny."

122

THE OXEN

CHRISTMAS EVE, and twelve of the clock.
    "Now they are all on their knees,"
An elder said as we sat in a flock
    By the embers in hearthside ease.

We pictured the meek mild creatures where
    They dwelt in their strawy pen,
Nor did it occur to one of us there
    To doubt they were kneeling then.

So fair a fancy few would weave
    In these years!   Yet, I feel,
If someone said on Christmas Eve,
    "Come; see the oxen kneel

In the lonely barton by yonder coomb
    Our childhood used to know,"
I should go with him in the gloom
    Hoping it might be so.

Thomas Hardy.

123

I SING OF A MAIDEN

I SING of a maiden
    That is makèles,
King of all kinges
    To her sone sche ches.

He cam al so stille
    There his moder was,
As dew in Aprille
    That falleth on the grass.
He cam al so stille
    To his moderes bour,
As dew in Aprille
    That falleth on the flour.
He cam al so stille
    There his moder lay,
As dew in Aprille
    That falleth on the spray.
Moder and maiden
    Was never non but sche;
Well may swich a lady
    Godès moder be.

15th Cent. MS.

124

THREE CAROLS

i

JOYS SEVEN

THE first good joy that Mary had,
    It was the joy of one;
To see the blessèd Jesus Christ
    When he was first her son:

When he was first her son, good man:
    And blessèd may he be,
Both Father, Son, and Holy Ghost,
    To all eternity.

The next good joy that Mary had,
    It was the joy of two;
To see her own son, Jesus Christ,
    To make the lame to go:

The next good joy that Mary had
    It was the joy of three;
To see her own son, Jesus Christ,
    To make the blind to see:

The next good joy that Mary had,
    It was the joy of four;
To see her own son, Jesus Christ,
    To read the Bible o'er.

The next good joy that Mary had,
    It was the joy of five;
To see her own son, Jesus Christ,
    To bring the dead alive:

The next good joy that Mary had,
    It was the joy of six;
To see her own son, Jesus Christ,
    Upon the crucifix:

The next good joy that Mary had,
    It was the joy of seven;
To see her own son, Jesus Christ,
    To wear the crown of heaven:

To wear the crown of heaven, good man,
    And blessèd may he be,
Both Father, Son, and Holy Ghost,
    To all eternity.

                             Traditional.

ii

THE HOLLY AND THE IVY

THE holly and the ivy,
When they are both full grown,
Of all the trees that are in the wood,
The holly bears the crown:

> *The rising of the sun*
> *And the running of the deer,*
> *The playing of the merry organ,*
> *Sweet singing in the choir.*

The holly bears a blossom,
As white as the lily flower,
And Mary bore sweet Jesus Christ,
To be our sweet Saviour.

The holly bears a berry,
As red as any blood,
And Mary bore sweet Jesus Christ
To do poor sinners good:

The holly bears a prickle,
As sharp as any thorn,
And Mary bore sweet Jesus Christ
On Christmas day in the morn:

The holly bears a bark,
As bitter as any gall,
And Mary bore sweet Jesus Christ
For to redeem us all:

The holly and the ivy,
When they are both full grown,
Of all the trees that are in the wood,
The holly bears the crown:

The rising of the sun
And the running of the deer,
The playing of the merry organ,
Sweet singing in the choir.

Traditional.

126

iii

THE COVENTRY CAROL

Lully, lulla, thou little tiny child,
By by, lully lullay.

O sisters too,
How may we do
    For to preserve this day
This poor youngling
For whom we do sing,
    By by, lully lullay?

Herod, the king,
In his raging,
    Chargèd he hath this day
His men of might,
In his own sight,
    All young childrén to slay.

That woe is me,
Poor child for thee!
    And ever morn and day

For thy parting
Neither say nor sing
    By by, lully lullay!

Lully, lulla, thou little tiny child,
By by, lully lullay.

15*th Century.*

From " The Pageant of the Shearmen and Tailors
   of Coventry."

127

A CONVERSATION

HE said, " No angels light the skies
Or thrill the world with song,
No Magi lift exultant eyes
Or haste the road along,
But stricken men with groans and sighs
Witness to hate and wrong."

The other answered, " Surely still
The shepherds watch their sheep?
And mothers, too, this evening thrill
To lull their babes asleep?
And through the clouds, athwart the hill
The bows their splendours keep?

The waters hold their ancient bounds,
And in the ancient fields
The reapers' age-old song resounds,
The flock its increase yields,
And simple loves and common rounds
From ill the spirit shields."

G. M. Miller.

TO MY SISTER

It is the first mild day of March:
Each minute sweeter than before
The redbreast sings from the tall larch
That stands beside our door.

There is a blessing in the air,
Which seems a sense of joy to yield
To the bare trees, and mountains bare,
And grass in the green field.

My sister! ('tis a wish of mine)
Now that our morning meal is done,
Make haste, your morning task resign;
Come forth and feel the sun.

Edward will come with you; and, pray,
Put on with speed your woodland dress;
And bring no book: for this one day
We'll give to idleness.

No joyless forms shall regulate
Our living calendar:
We from to-day, my Friend, will date
The opening of the year.

Love, now a universal birth,
From heart to heart is stealing.
From earth to man, from man to earth,
It is the hour of feeling.

One moment now may give us more
Than years of toiling reason:
Our minds shall drink at every pore
The spirit of the season.

Some silent laws our hearts will make,
Which they shall long obey:
We for the year to come may take
Our temper from to-day.

And from the blessed power that rolls
About, below, above,
We'll frame the measure of our souls:
They shall be tuned to love.

Then come, my Sister! come, I pray,
With speed put on your woodland dress;
And bring no book: for this one day
We'll give to idleness.

William Wordsworth.

129

WHAT ENDURES?

Nothing endures but personal qualities

WHAT do you think endures?
Do you think a great city endures?
Or a teeming manufacturing state? or a prepared constitution? or the best built steamships?
Or hotels of granite and iron? or any chefs-d'œuvre of engineering, forts, armaments?

Away! these are not to be cherished for themselves.
They fill their hour, the dancers dance, the musicians play for them,
The show passes, all does well enough of course,
All does very well till one flash of defiance.

A great city is that which has the greatest men and women.
If it be a few ragged huts, it is still the greatest city in the whole world.

Walt Whitman.

130

ON HIS BLINDNESS

WHEN I consider how my light is spent,
Ere half my days in this dark world and wide,
And that one talent which is death to hide,
Lodged with me useless, though my soul more bent
To serve therewith my Maker, and present
My true account, lest He returning chide—
Doth God exact day-labour, light denied?
I fondly ask; but Patience, to prevent
That murmur, soon replies, God doth not need
Either man's work or His own gifts: who best
Bear His mild yoke, they serve Him best; His state
Is kingly. Thousands at His bidding speed
And post o'er land and ocean without rest:
They also serve who only stand and wait.

John Milton.

131

ON THE LATE MASSACRE IN PIEDMONT

AVENGE, O Lord, thy slaughter'd saints, whose bones
Lie scattered on the Alpine mountains cold;
Even them who kept thy truth so pure of old,
When all our fathers worshipp'd stocks and stones,
Forget not! in thy book record their groans
Who were thy sheep, and in their ancient fold
Slain by the bloody Piedmontese that roll'd
Mother with infant down the rocks. Their moans
The vales redoubled to the hills, and they
To heaven. Their martyr'd blood and ashes sow

O'er all the Italian fields, where still doth sway
The triple tyrant; that from these may grow
A hundredfold, who, having learnt thy way,
Early may fly the Babylonian woe.

John Milton.

132

LONDON, 1802

MILTON! thou should'st be living at this hour:
England hath need of thee: she is a fen
Of stagnant waters: altar, sword, and pen,
Fireside, the heroic wealth of hall and bower,
Have forfeited their ancient English dower
Of inward happiness.   We are selfish men;
Oh! raise us up, return to us again;
And give us manners, virtue, freedom, power.
Thy soul was like a star, and dwelt apart:
Thou hadst a voice whose sound was like the sea,
Pure as the naked heavens, majestic, free;
So didst thou travel on life's common way
In cheerful godliness; and yet thy heart
The lowliest duties on herself did lay.

William Wordsworth.

133

THOUGHT OF A BRITON ON THE SUBJUGATION OF SWITZERLAND

Two Voices are there; one is of the sea,
One of the mountains; each a mighty Voice:
In both from age to age thou didst rejoice,
They were thy chosen music, Liberty!

There came a Tyrant, and with holy glee
Thou fought'st against him; but hast vainly striven:
Thou from thy Alpine holds at length art driven,
Where not a torrent murmurs heard by thee.
Of one deep bliss thine ear hath been bereft:
Then cleave, O cleave to that which still is left:
For, high-souled Maid, what sorrow would it be
That Mountain floods should thunder as before,
And Ocean bellow from his rocky shore,
And neither awful Voice be heard by thee!

William Wordsworth.

134

A TRIBUTE TO PITT, 1808

HAD'ST thou but lived, though stripped of power,
A watchman on the lonely tower,
Thy thrilling trump had roused the land
When fraud or danger were at hand;
By thee, as by the beacon-light,
Our pilots had kept course aright;
As some proud column, though alone,
Thy strength had propped the tottering throne:
Now is the stately column broke,
The beacon-light is quenched in smoke,
The trumpet's silver sound is still,
The warder silent on the hill!

From the Introduction to " Marmion,"
Sir Walter Scott.

135

ON THE CASTLE OF CHILLON

ETERNAL Spirit of the chainless Mind!
    Brightest in dungeons, Liberty, thou art—
    For there thy habitation is the heart—
The heart which love of thee alone can bind;

And when thy sons to fetters are consigned,
    To fetters, and the damp vault's dayless gloom,
    Their country conquers with their martyrdom,
And Freedom's fame finds wings on every wind.

Chillon! thy prison is a holy place
    And thy sad floor an altar, for 'twas trod,
(Until his very steps have left a trace
    Worn, as if thy cold pavement were a sod)
By Bonnivard!   May none those marks efface!
    For they appeal from tyranny to God.

Lord Byron.

136

A MYSTIC AS SOLDIER

I LIVED my days apart,
Dreaming fair songs for God,
By the glory in my heart
Covered and crowned and shod.

Now God is in the strife,
And I must seek Him there
Where death outnumbers life
And fury smites the air.

I walk the secret way
With anger in my brain.
O music through my clay,
When will you sound again?

Siegfried Sassoon.

137

ARMISTICE DAY, 1938

i

Twenty years this day I heard the last
Low monotone of guns defiant swell,
Then cease.   The four years' agony was past.
The unaccustomed silence, like a bell
Heard on the wold some Sabbath morning, seemed
To chime with silver sound.   The autumn air
Was crisp and keen: the quiet hillsides gleamed
With golden leaves under the branches bare.
　　It felt some dream too sweet for word or cry.
　　Rest, rest profound, for streams and woods and soil:
　　Till in a calm old age men came to die
　　In all these fields but hum of daily toil,
Only the wind the poplar branches sway,
Only the ploughshare rend the yielding clay!

ii

For twenty years the quiet fields have rested,
Only the scar of ploughs at seed-time borne,
For twenty years have yellowed unmolested
The patient squares of slowly ripening corn.
It was no dream that old November morning.
Beneath the poplars men have worked and sung,
Wooed and been happy, wed, and now watch dawning
Another happy manhood fair and young.

What tales are these? Dear God, can it be true
Those fields again must all be torn and battered,
Gray heads lose now the rest that is their due,
Those youthful limbs lie torment-racked and shattered,
Glad toil give place to devildoms obscene
As if that former day had never been?

G. M. Miller.

138

HUNGER

I COME among the peoples like a shadow.
I sit down by each man's side.

None sees me, but they look on one another,
And know that I am there.

My silence is like the silence of the tide
That buries the playground of children;

Like the deepening of frost in the slow night,
When birds are dead in the morning.

Armies trample, invade, destroy,
With guns roaring from earth and air.

I am more terrible than armies,
I am more feared than the cannon.

Kings and chancellors give commands;
I give no command to any;

But I am listened to more than kings
And more than passionate orators.

I unswear words, and undo deeds.
Naked things know me.

I am first and last to be felt of the living.
I am Hunger.

Laurence Binyon.

139

IN THESE OUR WINTER DAYS

In these our winter days
Death's iron tongue is glib
Numbing with fear all flesh upon
A fiery-hearted globe.

An age once green is buried,
Numbered the hours of light;
Blood-red across the snow our sun
Still trails his faint retreat.

Spring through death's iron guard
Her million blades shall thrust;
Love that was sleeping, not extinct,
Throw off the nightmare crust.

Eyes, though not ours, shall see
Sky-high a signal flame,
The sun returned to power above
A world, but not the same.

C. Day Lewis.

140

DAVID AND GOLIATH

LET Goliath have his say,
David won, and will to-day.
Let him wave his dreadful spear,
David lived, and now draws near.

See Goliath, mark his height!
What turns David on his might?
Valour lissom as a prayer
Running tiptoe up God's stair.

Scrip and sling and shepherd crook,
And five pebbles from the brook
David sets against his spear,
Shield and sword and armour gear.

See Goliath, where he lies
With the night upon his eyes!
All the winds of vale and hill
Chant of David and his skill.

Herbert E. Palmer.

141

IN TIME OF "THE BREAKING OF NATIONS"

ONLY a man harrowing clods
  In a slow silent walk
With an old horse that stumbles and nods
  Half asleep as they stalk.

Only thin smoke without flame
　　From the heaps of couch-grass:
Yet this will go onward the same
　　Though Dynasties pass.

Yonder a maid and her wight
　　Come whispering by:
War's annals will fade into night
　　Ere their story die.

Thomas Hardy.

142

BINNORIE

THERE were twa sisters sat in a bour;
　　Binnorie, O Binnorie!
There cam a knight to be their wooer,
　　By the bonnie milldams o' Binnorie.

He courted the eldest with glove and ring,
But he lo'ed the youngest abune a' thing.

The eldest she was vexèd sair,
And sair envied her sister fair.

Upon a morning fair and clear,
She cried upon her sister dear:

" O sister, sister, tak my hand,
And we'll see our father's ships to land."

She's ta'en her by the lily hand,
And led her down to the river-strand.

The youngest stood upon a stane,
The eldest cam and push'd her in.

" O sister, sister, reach your hand!
And ye sall be heir o' half my land:

" O sister, reach me but your glove!
And sweet William sall be your love."—

" Foul fa' the hand that I should take;
It twin'd me o' my warldis make.

" Your cherry cheeks and your yellow hair
Gar'd me gang maiden evermair."

Sometimes she sank, sometimes she swam,
Until she cam to the miller's dam.

Out then cam the miller's son,
And saw the fair maid soummin' in.

" O father, father, draw your dam!
There's either a mermaid or a milk-white swan."

The miller hasted and drew his dam,
And there he found a drown'd woman.

You couldna see her middle sma',
Her gowden girdle was sae braw.

You couldna see her lily feet,
Her gowden fringes were sae deep.

You couldna see her yellow hair
For the strings o' pearls were twisted there.

You couldna see her fingers sma',
Wi' diamond rings they were cover'd a'.

And by there cam a harper fine,
That harpit to the king at dine.

And when he look'd that lady on,
He sigh'd and made a heavy moan.

He's made a harp of her breast-bane,
Whose sound wad melt a heart of stane.

He's ta'en three locks o' her yellow hair,
And wi' them strung his harp sae rare.

He went into her father's hall,
And there was the court assembled all.

He laid his harp upon a stane,
And straight it began to play by lane:

" O yonder sits my father, the King,
And yonder sits my mother, the Queen;

" And yonder sits my brother Hugh,
And by him my William, sweet and true."

But the last tune that the harp play'd then—
    Binnorie, O Binnorie!
Was, " Woe to my sister, false Helèn! "
    By the bonnie milldams o' Binnorie.

Scottish Ballad.

143

MATIN SONG

PACK, clouds, away! and welcome, day
  With night we banish sorrow.
Sweet air, blow soft; mount, lark, aloft
  To give my Love good-morrow!
Wings from the wind to please her mind,
  Notes from the lark I'll borrow:
Bird, prune thy wing! nightingale, sing!
  To give my Love good-morrow!
      To give my Love good-morrow
      Notes from them all I'll borrow.

Wake from thy nest, robin red-breast!
  Sing, birds in every furrow!
And from each bill let music shrill
  Give my fair Love good-morrow!
Blackbird and thrush in every bush,
  Stare, linnet, and cocksparrow,
You pretty elves, among yourselves
  Sing my fair Love good-morrow!
      To give my Love good-morrow—
      Sing, birds, in every furrow!
                              Thomas Heywood.

144

LOVE SONG

MY luve is like a red red rose
  That's newly sprung in June:
My luve is like the melodie
  That's sweetly played in tune.

So fair art thou, my bonnie lass,
   So deep in luve am I;
And I will luve thee still, my dear,
   Till a' the seas gang dry.

Till a' the seas gang dry, my dear,
   And the rocks melt wi' the sun:
I will luve thee still, my dear,
   While the sands o' life shall run.

And fare thee weel, my only luve,
   And fare thee weel awhile!
And I will come again, my luve,
   Tho' it were ten thousand mile.

Robert Burns.

145

SONNET

WHEN, in disgrace with Fortune and men's eyes,
I all alone beweep my outcast state,
And trouble deaf heaven with my bootless cries,
And look upon myself, and curse my fate,
Wishing me like to one more rich in hope,
Featured like him, like him with friends possessed,
Desiring this man's art and that man's scope,
With what I most enjoy contented least;
Yet in these thoughts myself almost despising—
Haply I think on thee: and then my state,
Like to the lark at break of day arising
From sullen earth, sings hymns at Heaven's gate;
   For thy sweet love remembered such wealth brings
   That then I scorn to change my state with Kings.

William Shakespeare.

THE HIGHWAY

Highway, since you my chief Parnassus be,
And that my Muse, to some ears not unsweet,
Tempers her words to trampling horses' feet
More oft than to a chamber-melody,—
Now blessèd you bear onward blessèd me
To her, where I my heart, safe-left, shall meet;
My Muse and I must you of duty greet
With thanks and wishes, wishing thankfully;
Be you still fair, honoured by public heed;
By no encroachment wronged, nor time forgot;
Nor blamed for blood, nor shamed for sinful deed;
And that you know I envy you no lot
    Of highest wish, I wish you so much bliss,
    Hundreds of years you Stella's feet may kiss!
Sir Philip Sidney.

LOCHINVAR

O, young Lochinvar is come out of the west,
Through all the wide Border his steed was the best;
And save his good broadsword he weapons had none,
He rode all unarmed, and he rode all alone.
So faithful in love, and so dauntless in war,
There never was knight like the young Lochinvar.

He stayed not for brake, and he stopped not for stone,
He swam the Esk river where ford there was none;
But ere he alighted at Netherby gate,
The bride had consented, the gallant came late:

For a laggard in love, and a dastard in war,
Was to wed the fair Ellen of brave Lochinvar.

So boldly he entered the Netherby Hall,
Among bride's men, and kinsmen, and brothers, and all:
Then spoke the bride's father, his hand on his sword
(For the poor craven bridegroom said never a word),
" O come ye in peace here, or come ye in war,
Or to dance at our bridal, young Lord Lochinvar? "

" I long wooed your daughter, my suit you denied;—
Love swells like the Solway, but ebbs like its tide—
And now I am come, with this lost love of mine,
To lead but one measure, drink one cup of wine.
There are maidens in Scotland more lovely by far,
That would gladly be bride to the young Lochinvar."

The bride kissed the goblet: the knight took it up,
He quaffed off the wine, and he threw down the cup.
She looked down to blush, and she looked up to sigh,
With a smile on her lips, and a tear in her eye.
He took her soft hand, ere her mother could bar—
" Now tread we a measure! " said young Lochinvar.

So stately his form, and so lovely her face,
That never a hall such a galliard did grace;
While her mother did fret, and her father did fume,
And the bridegroom stood dangling his bonnet and plume;
And the bride-maidens whispered, " 'Twere better by far
To have matched our fair cousin with young Lochinvar."

One touch to her hand, and one word in her ear,
When they reached the hall-door, and the charger stood
    near:
So light to the croupe the fair lady he swung,
So light to the saddle before her he sprung!

" She is won! we are gone, over bank, bush, and scaur;
They'll have fleet steeds that follow," quoth young
  Lochinvar.

There was mounting 'mong Graemes of the Netherby clan;
Forsters, Fenwicks, and Musgraves, they rode and they ran:
There was racing and chasing on Cannobie Lee,
But the lost bride of Netherby ne'er did they see.
So daring in love, and so dauntless in war,
Have ye e'er heard of gallant like young Lochinvar?

Sir Walter Scott.

148

ROSABELLE

O LISTEN, listen, ladies gay!
  No haughty feat of arms I tell;
Soft is the note, and sad the lay
  That mourns the lovely Rosabelle.

—" Moor, moor the barge, ye gallant crew!
  And, gentle ladye, deign to stay!
Rest thee in Castle Ravensheuch,
  Nor tempt the stormy firth to-day.

" The blackening wave is edged with white:
  To inch and rock the sea-mews fly;
The fishers have heard the Water-Sprite,
  Whose screams forbode that wreck is nigh.

" Last night the gifted Seer did view
  A wet shroud swathed round ladye gay;
Then stay thee, fair, in Ravensheuch:
  Why cross the gloomy firth to-day? "

" 'Tis not because Lord Lindesay's heir
   To-night at Roslin leads the ball,
But that my ladye-mother there
   Sits lonely in her castle-hall.

" 'Tis not because the ring they ride,
   And Lindesay at the ring rides well,
But that my sire the wine will chide,
   If 'tis not fill'd by Rosabelle."—

O'er Roslin all that dreary night,
   A wondrous blaze was seen to gleam;
'Twas broader than the watch-fire's light,
   And redder than the bright moon-beam.

It glared on Roslin's castled rock,
   It ruddied all the copse-wood glen;
'Twas seen from Dryden's groves of oak,
   And seen from cavern'd Hawthornden.

Seem'd all on fire that chapel proud,
   Where Roslin's chiefs uncoffin'd lie,
Each Baron, for a sable shroud,
   Sheathed in his iron panoply.

Seem'd all on fire within, around,
   Deep sacristy and altar's pale;
Shone every pillar foliage-bound,
   And glimmer'd all the dead men's mail.

Blazed battlement and pinnet high,
   Blazed every rose-carved buttress fair—
So still they blaze, when fate is nigh
   The lordly line of high St. Clair.

There are twenty of Roslin's barons bold
  Lie buried within that proud chapelle;
Each one the holy vault doth hold—
  But the sea holds lovely Rosabelle!

And each St. Clair was buried there,
  With candle, with book, and with knell;
But the sea-caves rung, and the wild winds sung,
  The dirge of lovely Rosabelle.
                              Sir Walter Scott.

149

JOHN ANDERSON MY JO

JOHN ANDERSON my jo, John,
  When we were first acquent,
Your locks were like the raven,
  Your bonnie brow was brent;
But now your brow is beld, John,
  Your locks are like the snow;
But blessings on your frosty pow,
  John Anderson, my jo.

John Anderson my jo, John,
  We clamb the hill thegither;
And mony a canty day, John,
  We've had wi' ane anither:
Now we maun totter down, John,
  And hand in hand we'll go,
And sleep thegither at the foot,
  John Anderson, my jo.
                              Robert Burns.

150

LUCY

She dwelt among the untrodden ways
  Beside the springs of Dove,
A maid whom there were none to praise
  And very few to love:

A violet by a mossy stone
  Half hidden from the eye!
Fair as a star, when only one
  Is shining in the sky.

She lived unknown, and few could know
  When Lucy ceased to be;
But she is in her grave, and, oh,
  The difference to me!

William Wordsworth.

151

A SLUMBER

A slumber did my spirit seal;
  I had no human fears:
She seemed a thing that could not feel
  The touch of earthly years.

No motion has she now, no force;
  She neither hears nor sees;
Rolled round in earth's diurnal course,
  With rocks, and stones, and trees.

William Wordsworth.

ODE ON A GRECIAN URN

THOU still unravish'd bride of quietness,
   Thou foster-child of silence and slow time,
Sylvan historian, who canst thus express
   A flowery tale more sweetly than our rhyme:
What leaf-fring'd legend haunts about thy shape
   Of deities or mortals, or of both,
     In Tempe or the dales of Arcady?
   What men or gods are these?   What maidens loth?
What mad pursuit?   What struggle to escape?
     What pipes and timbrels?   What wild ecstasy?

Heard melodies are sweet, but those unheard
   Are sweeter; therefore, ye soft pipes, play on;
Not to the sensual ear, but, more endear'd,
   Pipe to the spirit ditties of no tone:
Fair youth, beneath the trees, thou canst not leave
   Thy song, nor ever can those trees be bare;
     Bold Lover, never, never canst thou kiss,
   Though winning near the goal—yet, do not grieve;
She cannot fade, though thou hast not thy bliss,
     For ever wilt thou love, and she be fair!

Ah, happy, happy boughs! that cannot shed
   Your leaves, nor ever bid the Spring adieu;
And, happy melodist, unwearièd,
   For ever piping songs for ever new;
More happy love! more happy, happy love!
   For ever warm and still to be enjoy'd,
     For ever panting, and for ever young;
All breathing human passion far above,
   That leaves a heart high-sorrowful and cloy'd,
     A burning forehead, and a parching tongue.

Who are these coming to the sacrifice?
  To what green altar, O mysterious priest,
Lead'st thou that heifer lowing at the skies,
  And all her silken flanks with garlands dressed?
What little town by river or sea shore,
  Or mountain-built with peaceful citadel,
    Is emptied of this folk, this pious morn?
And, little town, thy streets for evermore
    Will silent be; and not a soul to tell
      Why thou art desolate, can e'er return.

O Attic shape! Fair attitude! with brede
  Of marble men and maidens overwrought,
With forest branches and the trodden weed;
  Thou, silent form, dost tease us out of thought
As doth eternity: Cold Pastoral!
    When old age shall this generation waste,
    Thou shalt remain, in midst of other woe
Than ours, a friend to man, to whom thou say'st,
  "Beauty is truth, truth beauty,"—that is all
    Ye know on earth, and all ye need to know.
                                        John Keats.

153

INCIDENT OF THE FRENCH CAMP

You know, we French stormed Ratisbon:
  A mile or so away
On a little mound, Napoleon
  Stood on our storming-day;
With neck out-thrust, you fancy how,
  Legs wide, arms locked behind,
As if to balance the prone brow
  Oppressive with its mind.

Just as perhaps he mused " My plans
   That soar, to earth may fall,
Let once my army-leader Lannes
   Waver at yonder wall "—
Out 'twixt the battery-smokes there flew
   A rider, bound on bound
Full-galloping; nor bridle drew
   Until he reached the mound.

Then off there flung in smiling joy,
   And held himself erect
By just his horse's mane, a boy:
   You hardly could suspect—
(So tight he kept his lips compressed,
   Scarce any blood came through)
You looked twice ere you saw his breast
   Was all but shot in two.

" Well," cried he, " Emperor, by God's grace
   We've got you Ratisbon!
The Marshal's in the market-place,
   And you'll be there anon
To see your flag-bird flap his vans
   Where I, to heart's desire,
Perched him! " The Chief's eye flashed; his plans
   Soared up again like fire.

The Chief's eye flashed; but presently
   Softened itself, as sheathes
A film the mother-eagle's eye
   When her bruised eaglet breathes:
" You're wounded! " " Nay," his soldier's pride
   Touched to the quick, he said:
" I'm killed, Sire! " And his Chief beside,
   Smiling the boy fell dead.

Robert Browning.

THE LAST EXPLOIT OF SAMSON

MESSENGER.   Occasions drew me early to this city,
And, as the gates I enter'd with sun-rise,
The morning trumpets festival proclaimed
Through each high street.   Little I had despatch'd,
When all abroad was rumour'd that this day
Samson should be brought forth, to show the people
Proof of his mighty strength in feats and games;
I sorrow'd at his captive state, but minded
Not to be absent at that spectacle.
The building was a spacious theatre,
Half round on two main pillars vaulted high,
With seats, where all the lords, and each degree
Of sort, might sit in order to behold;
The other side was open, where the throng
On banks and scaffolds under sky might stand;
I among these aloof obscurely stood.
The feast and noon grew high, and sacrifice
Had fill'd their hearts with mirth, high cheer, and wine,
When to their sports they turned.   Immediately
Was Samson as a public servant brought,
In their state livery clad; before him pipes
And timbrels, on each side went armèd guards,
Both horse and foot before him, and behind
Archers, and slingers, cataphracts, and spears.
At sight of him the people with a shout
Rifted the air, clamouring their god with praise,
Who had made their dreadful enemy their thrall.
He, patient but undaunted where they led him,
Came to the place, and what was set before him,
Which without help of eye might be essay'd,
To heave, pull, draw, or break, he still perform'd
All with incredible stupendous force,

None daring to appear antagonist.
At length, for intermission's sake, they led him
Between the pillars; he his guide requested,
For so from such as nearer stood we heard,
As over-tired, to let him lean awhile
With both his arms on those two massy pillars,
That to the archèd roof gave main support.
He unsuspicious led him; which, when Samson
Felt in his arms, with head awhile inclined,
And eyes fast fix'd, he stood, as one who pray'd,
Or some great matter in his mind revolved:
At last, with head erect, thus cried aloud:
Hitherto, lords, what your commands imposed
I have perform'd, as reason was, obeying,
Not without wonder or delight beheld:
Now, of my own accord, such other trial
I mean to show you of my strength, yet greater;
As with amaze shall strike all who behold.
This utter'd, straining all his nerves, he bow'd.
As with the force of winds and waters pent,
When mountains tremble, those two massy pillars
With horrible convulsion to and fro
He tugg'd, he shook, till down they came, and drew
The whole roof after them, with burst of thunder
Upon the heads of all who sat beneath,
Lords, ladies, captains, counsellors, or priests,
Their choice nobility and flower, not only
Of this, but each Philistian city round,
Met from all parts to solemnise this feast.
Samson, with these immix'd, inevitably
Pull'd down the same destruction on himself;
The vulgar only 'scaped who stood without.

   .   .   .   .

MANOA. Come, come, no time for lamentation now,
Nor much more cause: Samson hath quit himself

Like Samson, and heroically hath finish'd
A life heroic, on his enemies
Fully revenged, hath left them years of mourning,
And lamentation to the sons of Caphtor
Through all Philistian bounds.   To Israel
Honour hath left, and freedom, let but them
Find courage to lay hold on this occasion;
To himself and father's house eternal fame;
And, which is best and happiest yet, all this
With God not parted from him, as was fear'd,
But favouring and assisting to the end.
Nothing is here for tears, nothing to wail
Or knock the breast, no weakness, no contempt,
Dispraise, or blame, nothing but well and fair,
And what may quiet us in a death so noble.

·   ·   ·   ·

CHORUS.   All is best, though we oft doubt
What the unsearchable dispose
Of highest wisdom brings about,
And ever best found in the close.
Oft he seems to hide his face,
But unexpectedly returns,
And to his faithful champion hath in place
Bore witness gloriously; whence Gaza mourns,
And all that band them to resist
His uncontrollable intent;
His servants he, with new acquist
Of true experience from this great event,
With peace and consolation hath dismiss'd,
And calm of mind, all passion spent.

From " Samson Agonistes,"
John Milton.

TWO EPISODES FROM "PARADISE LOST"

i. SATAN

HE trusted to have equalled the Most High,
If he opposed; and, with ambitious aim
Against the throne and monarchy of God,
Raised impious war in heaven, and battle proud,
With vain attempt.   Him the Almighty Power
Hurl'd headlong flaming from the ethereal sky
With hideous ruin and combustion, down
To bottomless perdition, there to dwell
In adamantine chains and penal fire,
Who durst defy the Omnipotent to arms.

    .   .   .   .

                        He, above the rest
In shape and gesture proudly eminent,
Stood like a tower; his form had not yet lost
All its original brightness, nor appear'd
Less than archangel ruin'd, and the excess
Of glory obscured: as when the sun new-risen
Looks through the horizontal misty air,
Shorn of his beams; or from behind the moon
In dim eclipse, disastrous twilight sheds
On half the nations, and with fear of change
Perplexes monarchs: darken'd so, yet shone
Above them all the archangel; but his face
Deep scars of thunder had intrench'd, and care
Sat on his faded cheek, but under brows
Of dauntless courage, and considerate pride
Waiting revenge: cruel his eye, but cast
Signs of remorse and passion to behold
The fellows of his crime, the followers rather,
Far other once beheld in bliss, condemn'd

For ever now to have their lot in pain,
Millions of spirits for his fault amerced
Of heaven, and from eternal splendours flung
For his revolt, yet faithful how they stood,
Their glory wither'd: as when heaven's fire
Hath scathed the forest oaks or mountain pines
With singèd top, their stately growth, though bare,
Stands on the blasted heath.   He now prepared
To speak; whereat their doubled ranks they bend
From wing to wing, and half enclose him round
With all his peers: attention held them mute.
Thrice he essay'd, and thrice in spite of scorn
Tears, such as angels weep, burst forth: at last
Words interwove with sighs found out their way.

156

ii. SATAN, GUIDED BY CHAOS, WINS HIS FIRST
SIGHT OF EARTH

THUS Satan; and him thus the Anarch old,
With faltering speech and visage incomposed,
Answer'd: I know thee, stranger, who thou art,
That mighty leading angel, who of late
Made head 'gainst heaven's King, though overthrown.
I saw and heard; for such a numerous host
Fled not in silence through the frighted deep,
With ruin upon ruin, rout on rout,
Confusion worse confounded; and heaven-gates
Poured out by millions her victorious bands
Pursuing.   I upon my frontiers here
Keep residence; if all I can will serve
That little which is left so to defend,
Encroached on still through your intestine broils
Weakening the sceptre of old Night: first hell,

Your dungeon, stretching far and wide beneath;
Now lately heaven and earth, another world,
Hung o'er my realm, link'd in a golden chain
To that side heaven from whence your legions fell:
If that way be your walk, you have not far;
So much the nearer danger; go and speed;
Havoc, and spoil, and ruin are my gain.

He ceased; and Satan stay'd not to reply,
But, glad that now his sea should find a shore,
With fresh alacrity and force renew'd
Springs upward, like a pyramid of fire,
Into the wild expanse, and, through the shock
Of fighting elements, on all sides round
Environ'd, wins his way; harder beset
And more endanger'd, than when Argo pass'd
Through Bosphorus betwixt the justling rocks:
Or when Ulysses on the starboard shunn'd
Charybdis, and by the other whirlpool steer'd.
So he with difficulty and labour hard
Moved on, with difficulty and labour he;
But he once pass'd, soon after when man fell,
Strange alteration!   Sin and Death amain
Following his track, such was the will of Heaven,
Paved after him a broad and beaten way
Over the dark abyss, whose boiling gulf
Tamely endured a bridge of wondrous length,
From hell continued, reaching the utmost orb
Of this frail world; by which the spirits perverse
With easy intercourse pass to and fro
To tempt or punish mortals, except whom
God and good angels guard by special grace.
But now at last the sacred influence
Of light appears, and from the walls of heaven
Shoots far into the bosom of dim Night
A glimmering dawn: here Nature first begins
Her farthest verge, and Chaos to retire,

As from her outmost works, a broken foe,
With tumult less, and with less hostile din,
That Satan with less toil and now with ease
Wafts on the calmer wave by dubious light,
And, like a weather-beaten vessel, holds
Gladly the port, though shrouds and tackle torn;
Or in the emptier waste, resembling air,
Weighs his spread wings, at leisure to behold
Far off the empyreal heaven, extended wide
In circuit, undetermined square or round,
With opal towers and battlements adorn'd
Of living sapphire, once his native seat;
And fast by, hanging in a golden chain,
This pendant world, in bigness as a star
Of smallest magnitude close by the moon.
Thither, full fraught with mischievous revenge,
Accursed, and in a cursèd hour, he hies.

John Milton.

157

TO MR. LAWRENCE

LAWRENCE, of virtuous father virtuous son,
Now that the fields are dank, and ways are mire,
Where shall we sometimes meet, and by the fire
Help waste a sullen day? what may be won
From the hard season gaining? Time will run
On smoother, till Favonius reinspire
The frozen earth, and clothe in fresh attire
The lily and the rose, that neither sowed nor spun.
What neat repast shall feast us, light and choice,
Of Attic taste, with wine, whence we may rise
To hear the lute well touched, or artful voice

Warble immortal notes and Tuscan air?
He who of those delights can judge, and spare
To interpose them oft, is not unwise.

John Milton.

158

TO A POET A THOUSAND YEARS HENCE

I WHO am dead a thousand years,
   And wrote this sweet archaic song,
Send you my words for messengers
   The way I shall not pass along.

I care not if you bridge the seas,
   Or ride secure the cruel sky,
Or build consummate palaces
   Of metal or of masonry.

But have you wine and music still,
   And statues and a bright-eyed love,
And foolish thoughts of good and ill,
   And prayers to them who sit above?

How shall we conquer? Like a wind
   That falls at eve our fancies blow,
And old Maeonides the blind
   Said it three thousand years ago.

O friend unseen, unborn, unknown,
   Student of our sweet English tongue,
Read out my words at night, alone:
   I was a poet, I was young.

Since I can never see your face,
    And never shake you by the hand,
I send my soul through time and space
    To greet you.   You will understand.
                                    James Elroy Flecker.

159

AFTER-THOUGHT

I THOUGHT of thee, my partner and my guide,
As being passed away.—Vain sympathies!
For, backward, Duddon! as I cast my eyes,
I see what was, and is, and will abide;
Still glides the Stream, and shall for ever glide;
The Form remains, the Function never dies;
While we, the brave, the mighty, and the wise,
We Men, who in our morn of youth defied
The elements, must vanish;—be it so!
Enough, if something from our hands have power
To live, and act, and serve the future hour;
And if, as toward the silent tomb we go,
Through love, through hope, and faith's transcendent
    dower,
We feel that we are greater than we know.
                                    William Wordsworth.

160

LET US NOW PRAISE FAMOUS MEN

LET us now praise famous men, and our fathers that begat us.
    The Lord hath wrought great glory by them through his
great power from the beginning.

Such as did bear rule in their kingdoms, men renowned for their power, giving counsel by their understanding, and declaring prophecies:

Leaders of the people by their counsels, and by their knowledge of learning meet for the people, wise and eloquent in their instructions:

Such as found out musical tunes, and recited verses in writing:

Rich men furnished with ability, living peaceably in their habitations:

All these were honoured in their generations, and were the glory of their times.

There be of them, that have left a name behind them, that their praises might be reported.

And some there be which have no memorial; who are perished as though they had never been; and are become as though they had never been born; and their children after them.

But these were merciful men, whose righteousness hath not been forgotten.

With their seed shall continually remain a good inheritance, and their children are within the covenant.

Their seed standeth fast, and their children for their sakes.

Their seed shall remain for ever, and their glory shall not be blotted out.

Their bodies are buried in peace; but their name liveth for evermore.

From the Apocrypha.

161

LOVE

Love bade me welcome; yet my soul drew back,
    Guilty of dust and sin.
But quick-eyed Love, observing me grow slack
    From my first entrance in,

Drew nearer to me; sweetly questioning,
    If I lacked anything.

" A guest," I answered, " worthy to be here "—
    Love said, " You shall be he."
" I, the unkind, ungrateful?   Ah! my dear,
    I cannot look on thee."
Love took my hand; and, smiling, did reply,
    " Who made the eyes, but I? "

" Truth, Lord; but I have marred them: let my shame
    Go where it doth deserve."
" And know you not," says Love, " who bore the blame? "
    " My dear, then I will serve."
" You must sit down," says Love, " and taste my meat."
    So I did sit and eat.

George Herbert.

162

WONDER AND PRAISE

OH, that men would praise the Lord for his goodness,
And for his wonderful works to the children of men!

And let them sacrifice the sacrifices of thanksgiving
And declare his works with rejoicing.

They that go down to the sea in ships,
That do business in great waters;

These see the works of the Lord,
And his wonders in the deep.

For he commandeth, and raiseth the stormy wind,
Which lifteth up the waves thereof.

They mount up to the heaven, they go down again to the
   depths:
Their soul is melted because of trouble.

They reel to and fro, and stagger like a drunken man,
And are at their wit's end.

Then they cry unto the Lord in their trouble,
And he bringeth them out of their distresses.

He maketh the storm a calm,
So that the waves thereof are still.

Then are they glad because they be quiet;
So he bringeth them unto their desired haven.

From Psalm 107.

INDEX OF FIRST LINES

(The numbers of the poems only are given)